商务英语专业"互联网+"创新型教材

2018年第一批教育部——开元电子产学合作协同育人项目——"应用型本科院校商务英语专业创新创业一体化人才培养模式研究"成果之一（项目编号：201801222045）

2018教育部——北京数通国软产学合作协同育人项目——"应用型本科院校商务英语专业课程体系'需求分析'模型的构建"研究成果之一（项目编号：201801148010）

外贸英语函电写作教程

主　编　蒋景东　宋秀峰　陈国雄
副主编　朱玉琴　谭　兴　张　坚
参　编　郭艳红　项　燕　何冬云
　　　　李　莉　赖海威　汤文瑞
　　　　伍　凤　陀子荣
主　审　司汝军

机械工业出版社

本书是校企合作开发教材，按照国际贸易流程编写，分 7 个情境，共 24 个单元，内容涉及外贸英语函电绪论，建立贸易关系，询盘、报盘和还盘，订单和合同，支付方式，装运和保险，申诉和索赔。

本书在每个情境中提出本情境的学习目标，并介绍相关写作知识。学习目标和情境介绍为每个情境一个，与之对应（Situation 1—Introductory Remarks 之外），在本情境所有任务讲解完毕之后，增加总结（Sum-Up），主要归纳各个情境的典型句式等。每个情境包括若干任务，在每个任务单元中都包括四个部分即 Preparing, Performing, Practicing 和 Supplement 部分。Preparing 部分包括本单元相关写作知识阅读和对话两个方面的内容，即 Relative Reading 和 Lead In—Dialogues。Performing 包括写作的具体内容（案例）和注解，即 Text（Sample）和 Notes。Practicing 包括翻译和写作等实训内容。Supplement 包括 Supplementary Reading（补充阅读部分）和 Knowledge Link（知识链接）两个部分。

本书既可以作为独立的外贸英语函电写作实训教材使用，也可作为相关国际商务专业配套教材使用，适合应用型本科院校和高职高专院校的学生学习，也适合所有想学外贸英语函电写作的人群学习。

为方便教学，本书配有**电子课件**，凡选用本书作为教材的教师均可登录机械工业出版社教材服务网 www.cmpedu.com 免费下载。本书还配备了丰富的**延伸阅读**内容，读者只需扫一扫书中的二维码，即可轻松阅读。如有问题，请致电 010-88379375 咨询。

图书在版编目（CIP）数据

外贸英语函电写作教程 / 蒋景东，宋秀峰，陈国雄主编. —北京：机械工业出版社，2018.12

商务英语专业"互联网+"创新型教材

ISBN 978-7-111-61444-9

Ⅰ.①外… Ⅱ.①蒋… ②宋… ③陈… Ⅲ.①对外贸易-英语-电报信函-写作-教材 Ⅳ.①F75

中国版本图书馆 CIP 数据核字（2018）第 262403 号

机械工业出版社（北京市百万庄大街 22 号　邮政编码 100037）
策划编辑：杨晓昱　　责任编辑：杨晓昱　徐梦然　张美杰
版式设计：张文贵　　责任校对：张文贵
责任印制：张　博
河北鑫兆源印刷有限公司印刷
2019 年 2 月第 1 版第 1 次印刷
184mm×260mm・13.75 印张・310 千字
0 001—3 000 册
标准书号：ISBN 978-7-111-61444-9
定价：36.00 元

凡购本书，如有缺页、倒页、脱页，由本社发行部调换

电话服务	网络服务
服务咨询热线：010-88379833	机 工 官 网：www.cmpbook.com
读者购书热线：010-88379649	机 工 官 博：weibo.com/cmp1952
	教育服务网：www.cmpedu.com
封面无防伪标均为盗版	金 书 网：www.golden-book.com

前 言

"外贸英语函电写作"课程的主旨是培养涉外商务英语专业人才、国际贸易专业人才和国际商务专业人才，满足市场对其各个方面的需求。因此，我们编写本书以培养学生通过外贸函电写作去处理实际商务问题的能力。

无论商务英语专业、国际贸易专业还是国际商务专业，在涉外商务活动中都是"商务知识+语言实践+交际技能+文化背景知识"的综合，需要科学性与艺术性相结合，这大大增加了外贸英语函电写作实训的力度。"外贸英语函电写作教程"这门课主要是培养涉外商务活动中的写作交际技能，如果没有大量亲身参与实践，这些技能是无法培养的。写作交际实践具有很强的灵活性、艺术性和权变性，这些是无法用传统说教方式再现的。本书在传统外贸英语函电教材的基础上，通过"互联网+"的方法来体现，利用信息通信技术以及互联网平台，让互联网与商务英语教学、国际贸易教学和国际商务教学进行深度融合，创造新的外贸英语函电写作教学。它是一种新的外贸英语函电教学形式，即充分发挥互联网在商务英语教学、国际贸易教学和国际商务教学中的优化和集成作用，将商务英语教学、国际贸易教学和国际商务教学互联网的创新成果进行深化。

基于以上考虑，本书编者遵循了下列编写原则和思路：

1. 突出专业教育的特点，使外贸函电写作知识条理化、系统化。根据商务英语专业人才、国际贸易专业人才和国际商务专业人才的培养目标，本书的内容涵盖对外贸易活动的各个层面，内容包括绪论部分（商务信函的格式、结构和写作的过程及写作原则），建立贸易关系，询盘、报盘和还盘，订单和合同，支付方式，装运和保险，申诉和索赔。

2. 任务驱动，有针对性地体现"实用"。根据情境设置任务，突出任务的技能与训练。

3. 突出专业知识的实用阅读。在每个写作任务之前和之后，都安排了相关的专业知识阅读，扩大学生专业知识的层面，避免学习过程中忽视知识拓展的弊端。

4. 突出实践性。在每一个任务学习之前，通过和本单元写作内容相关的阅读和对话引出要学习的专业内容，具有实用性和可操作性的特点。而且，在写作样章学习结束之后，每个任务都相应地安排了实训的内容，具有情境性、趣味性和可模拟性的特点。

5. 突出"互联网+"与外贸函电教学融合的特点。在每个情境的内容中都设有二维码，不受时间和空间的限制，以便学生学习和巩固。

本书的编写是我们编委的又一次尝试，是在体现商务英语专业、国际贸易专业和国际商务专业这一职场大方向的职业教育要求中，为满足市场需求所做出的努力。本书的编写完全按照应用型本科院校商务英语专业人才、国际贸易专业人才和国际商务专业人才培养的目标建设运作，教材编写的理念、组织形式和运作方式等进行了一系列的更新和创新。本书的编写主要突出了以下的教学理念：

1. 为外经贸和涉外企事业单位培养具有开阔视野的应用型专门人才；
2. 为外经贸和涉外企事业单位培养具有扎实语言基本功的专门人才；
3. 为外经贸和涉外企事业单位培养掌握系统商务知识的应用型专门人才；
4. 为外经贸和涉外企事业单位培养具有较强跨文化交际能力的应用型专门人才；
5. 为外经贸和涉外企事业单位培养具有团队协作精神的应用型专门人才。

本书结合作者多年的教学经验和商务经验，以商务英语专业人才、国际贸易专业人才和国际商务专业人才的培养目标为基准，借鉴国内外的先进教学方法，结合教学实际，设计了系统的外贸函电写作实训体系，以情境教学引领、单元任务作为基本逻辑框架，将职场交际理念与语言综合训练结合，每个写作实训任务都采用了目前流行的、颇受学生欢迎的准环境下的仿真模拟训练。

本书分7个情境，共24个单元，内容涉及外贸英语函电绪论，建立贸易关系，询盘、报盘和还盘，订单和合同，支付方式，装运和保险，申诉和索赔。

本书在每个情境中提出本情境的学习目标和本情境相关写作知识的介绍。学习目标和情境介绍为每个情境一个，与之对应（Situation 1—Introductory Remarks 之外），在本情境所有任务讲解完毕之后，增加总结（Sum-Up），主要归纳各个情境的典型句式等。每个情境包括若干任务，在每个任务单元中都包括四个部分即 Preparing，Performing，Practicing 和 Supplement 部分。Preparing 部分包括本单元相关写作知识阅读和对话两个方面的内容，即 Relative Reading 和 Lead In—Dialogues。Performing 包括写作的具体内容（案例）和注解，即 Text（Sample）和 Notes。Practicing 包括翻译和写作等实训内容。Supplement 包括 Supplementary Reading（补充阅读部分）和 Knowledge Link（知识链接）两个部分。各个部分的功能如下。

1. Preparing：Relative Reading 和 Lead In—Dialogues（相关写作知识阅读和对话导入）

相关写作知识阅读部分使学生先行了解所要学习的内容，而对话导入部分则使学生如临其境，更易于接受本任务中所要学习的内容。

2. Performing：Text（Sample）和 Notes（信函样例和注释）

信函样例和注释部分给学生模拟仿真练习打下坚实基础。

3. Practicing（实训练习）

实训练习有助于提升学生的学习积极性，同时突出了本课程的实用性和实践性，以此培养学生对信函写作知识的运用能力和具体操作能力。

4. Supplement：Supplementary Reading 和 Knowledge Links（补充阅读和知识链接）

补充阅读部分主要包含相应的信函示例以及相关文章以便学生课后阅读，进一步强化 Performing 部分中所学的内容。知识链接部分主要介绍课文中涉及的或可能涉及的相关的商务知识，帮助学生理解所学的内容，有助于提升学生的综合商务素养，拓展学生的知识层面。

本书内容对学生在商务环境下的职场交际能力和表达能力进行训练。书中附录包含大量的商务交际活动中的交际语言和词汇，可使学生的模拟仿真实训能力进一步提升。

此外，本书从培养学生的职业迁移能力出发，以培养21世纪国际通用性商务人才为目的，对传统的教材进行改革和创新，创新点如下：

1. 教学理念上的创新。以学生为本，凸显"导"字，通过Preparing进行引导，进行参与式教学，教师从主讲人、管理者变为导演者、导游者、导航者，学生不再是教师灌输知识的被动接收者、被监督者，而是全面参与教学设计和自我管理的课堂主人，充分体现了"教、学、做"合一的理念。

2. 教学内容上的创新。本书的内容以商务活动外贸函电写作用语为导向，内容情景化，每个单元内容以能力培养为主导，以职业技能需求细化分析为根据，以满足岗位技能要求为目标，构建"教、学、做"一体化的内容体系，培养学生的外贸函电写作交际能力和处理经贸实务问题的语言写作应用能力，以适应社会对国际商务从业人员的素质要求。

3. 教学方式上的创新。创建学习团队，由学生们组建学习团队，自主学习、集体学习、相互学习；通过各种生动活泼的方式构建互动式课堂；创造各种由学生全面参与式的亲验教学，把教学的时空视野从课堂内扩大到课堂外，实现教学渠道与空间的多元化与立体化。

4. 教学目标上的创新。注重三维目标，即知识与技能、过程与方法、情感态度与价值观，体现了显性教学和隐性教学相结合的原则。

5. 教学体系上的创新。建立学生全面参与的教学体系，从教学理念、教学组织形式，到多媒体教学、系列化信函写作实训、全过程开放，构建了由学生参与的、立体化、系统化的系统。

6. 教学方法上的创新。本书采用二维码的教学方法，在每个情境中增设"扫一扫，看延伸阅读内容"的部分，提供外贸英语函电写作的延伸知识，突出"互联网＋"在外贸英语函电教学中的应用，满足学生学习需求，使外贸英语函电教学更具有互动性，同时优化了外贸英语函电教学的知识结构，使知识更具有合理性。在此基础上扩展了外贸英语函电教学的范围，使外贸英语函电教学更具有无边界性，这种无边界性改变了学生的学习行为，使学习具有分享性，丰富了学生学习外贸英语函电写作知识的信息，使学生的学习具有自主性。

本书集应用型本科院校和国家示范性高职建设院校的教学、科研之所长。参与本书编写的院校有本科院校"贺州学院"和国家示范性高职建设院校"安徽机电职业技术学院"。

本书主编由贺州学院的蒋景东、陈国雄以及闽江学院的宋秀峰担任；副主编由贺州学院的朱玉琴，谭兴和张坚担任；贺州学院的郭艳红、何冬云、李莉、赖海威、汤文瑞、伍凤、陀子荣以及安徽机电职业技术学院的项燕参加编写。

本书是2018年第一批教育部——开元电子产学合作协同育人项目——"应用型本科院校商务英语专业创新创业一体化人才培养模式研究"成果之一（项目编号：201801222045）；

2018年教育部——北京数通国软产学合作协同育人项目——"应用型本科院校商务英语专业课程体系'需求分析'模型的构建"研究成果之一（项目编号：201801148010）。

本书强调外贸英语函电专业语言的使用和能力培养，突出实训，强调外贸函电写作专业知识和外贸语言的整体性及情境性，注重可操作性和模拟性。本书既可以作为独立的外贸英语函电写作实训教材使用，也可作为相关国际商务专业的配套教材作用，适合应用型本科院校和高职高专院校的学生学习，也适合所有想学外贸英语函电写作的人群学习。

本书在编写过程中，参阅了目前已经出版的国内外优秀教材、专著和相关资料，引用了一些有关的内容和研究成果，恕不一一详尽说明，仅在参考文献中列出，在此向有关作者致以衷心的感谢！

限于作者水平有限，书中难免有错误和不妥之处，敬请各位读者不吝赐教！

编　者

Contents

前言

Situation 1　Introductory Remarks ············ 1
　　Task 1　Form of Business Letters ············ 2
　　Task 2　Structure of Business Letters ············ 6
　　Task 3　The Process and Writing Principles of Business Letters ············ 20
　　延伸阅读 ············ 32

Situation 2　Establishing Business Relations ············ 33
　　Task 1　The First Communication from the Seller ············ 34
　　Task 2　The First Communication from the Buyer ············ 40
　　Task 3　Credit Inquiry ············ 46
　　延伸阅读 ············ 56

Situation 3　Negotiations and Consultations ············ 57
　　Task 1　General Enquiry and Reply ············ 58
　　Task 2　Specific Enquiry and Reply ············ 67
　　Task 3　Firm Offer ············ 76
　　Task 4　Non-Firm Offer ············ 84
　　Task 5　Counter-Offer ············ 90
　　延伸阅读 ············ 98

Situation 4　Conclusion of Business and the Fulfillment of a Contract ············ 99
　　Task 1　Orders and Acknowledgement ············ 100
　　Task 2　Acceptance or Rejection of Orders ············ 106
　　Task 3　Sending Contracts ············ 115
　　延伸阅读 ············ 124

Situation 5　Terms of Payment 125
　　Task 1　Suggesting a Certain Term of Payment 126
　　Task 2　Asking for an Easy Payment 134
　　Task 3　Urging Establishment of L/C 141
　　Task 4　Asking for Amendment to L/C 148
　　Task 5　Asking for Extension of L/C 155
　　延伸阅读 161

Situation 6　Shipment and Insurance 162
　　Task 1　Packing Requirements 163
　　Task 2　Shipment 171
　　Task 3　Insurance 180
　　延伸阅读 188

Situation 7　Complaints and Claims 189
　　Task 1　Complaints and Reply 190
　　Task 2　Claims and Settlement 198
　　延伸阅读 208
　　常见外贸英语函电写作模板 208

参考文献 209

Reading makes a full man;
Conference, a ready man;
Writing, an exact man.

读书使人丰富；
讨论使人成熟；
写作使人精确。

Situation 01: Introductory Remarks

🖊 Objectives

1. To know the parts and structures of business letters.
2. To know the layout of business letters.
3. To understand the writing principles and language characteristics of business letters.

🖊 Introduction

With the rapid development of the economic globalization and the constant increase of economic activities in the world, business letters have become one of the most effective and constantly used means of communication in international trade. Its main function is to inform or remind the counterpart or the public of a certain thing and also ask them to act according to the rules written in the letters.

Nowadays, although conventional letters are used less and less, millions of business letters are being sent by fax or e-mail to carry out business routine, such as E-commerce involving offering, ordering, enquiring, payment and complaints. All these are on the basis of writing skills in business letters. Good writing may lead you to gain more opportunities, otherwise bad writing may cause misunderstanding, conflicts, even miserable business war. So when you are writing business letters, you should be careful enough to express your meanings in correct words and expressions. This unit is intended to develop skills in writing such good business letters.

Requirements for the Language

- Accurate: correct facts and details
- Brief: short, simple, non-technical
- Clear: easy, natural, avoid formality

- Logic: "4-point plan"
- Empathetic: in reader's place
- Right: proofread spelling and facts

Task 1 Form of Business Letters

Preparing

 Relative Reading

The Essence of Business Letters

Every business letter communicates in two distinct ways. The reader gets meaning out of what is said and how it is said in a letter. This kind of communication is not at all peculiar only to business letters. In any face-to-face conversation, for example, a person's manner of speaking, the smile or frown on his face, the tone of the voice and etc., all tell something beyond what the words say. This "implied" message can either reinforce or contradict the words. It is the same case with business letters. The combination of a central message and an implied message is the total message a reader gets from reading that letter.

What is the importance of this concept of a double message? Considered in its most fundamental terms, a business letter may be defined as a message that attempts to influence its recipient to take some action or attitude desired by the sender. This desired result may be of immediate importance, such as the collecting of a bill, or just an intangible attitude like goodwill. Therefore, we must make sure that both the clarity of the message (what the letter says) and its character (how the letter says it) help to evoke that reaction. In other words, we need to make sure the implied message works for rather than against our purposes.

Performing

 Layout of a Business Letter

There are three main layouts of the business letter: indented style, blocked style and combined style.

1. Indented Style（缩进式）

Indented style is the traditional British practice with the heading usually in the middle and the date on the right-hand side. The main feature in this style is that each line of the "inside name and address", should be indented 2-3 spaces, and the first line of each paragraph should be 3-8 spaces. The complimentary close and signature may be in the center or commence at the center point. The first line of each paragraph should be indented.

```
                          Letterhead
Reference Number
                                                              Date

Inside Name and Address
Attention
Salutation
                         Subject Line
Message
-------------------------------------------------------------------
-------------------------------------------------------------------
                                                 Complimentary Close
                                                          Signature
Enclosure
Carbon Copy
Postscript
```

2. Blocked Style（齐头式）

Every line in the full block style begins at the left margin, and the open style of punctuation has been adopted. It is the most popular practice of displaying business letters. Its remarkable feature is that all typing lines, including those for the date, the inside name and address, the salutation, the subject heading, each message paragraph and the complimentary close, begin at the left-hand margin.

The end of the date line, the inside address lines, the salutation, the complimentary close and the signature lines are unpunctuated, but a comma is necessary between the day and year in the date line and the full stop is retained after the abbreviation such as company,

Inc. and Ltd.

```
                              Letterhead
Reference Number
Date
Inside Name and Address
Attention
Salutation
Subject Line
Message
--------------------------------------------------------------
--------------------------------------------------------------
Complimentary Close
Signature
Enclosure
Carbon Copy
Postscript
```

3. Combined Style（混合式）

Combined style is the mixture of the above two styles. The letterhead is usually in the middle. The first line of a paragraph is lined up with the left margin, but the date, the closing and the signature are indented.

✓ Envelop Addressing

There are two basic requirements of envelop addressing: accuracy and clearness.

Example

```
Shanghai Sunlight Chemical Product Co. Ltd.
38 Huaihai Road
Shanghai
China
                              President John Gates
                              Pacific Standard Trade Corp.
                              43 Queensway
                              London
                              U. K.
```

Practicing

I. Translate the following from English to Chinese.

form of business letters
three main layouts of the business letter
blocked style
traditional British practice
on the right-hand side
commence at the center point
the most popular practice
remarkable feature
begin at the left-hand margin
combined style is the mixture of the above two styles
the first line of a paragraph is lined up with the left margin
date, closing and signature
basic requirements

layout of business letter
indented style
combined style
in the middle
in the center
the first line of each paragraph
displaying business communications
all typing lines

envelop addressing
accuracy and clearness

II. Translate the following Chinese business letters into English and analyze the form of these letters.

1. 要求修改信用证信函

周先生：

事由：158号信用证

你方第121号订单，8公吨核桃仁，金额计2 660美元标题项下的信用证已收到，谢谢。

然而,我们很遗憾地告知你方信用证中有一处与合同规定不符。你方信用证金额未开足,因为你方订单正确的CIF(到岸价格)总值应是2,960美元,而不是2,660美元,这之间相差了300美元之多。为了使我们能及时发货,请立即用传真修改你方信用证,并将信用证金额增加到2,960美元。一接到你方传真修改的信用证,我们将立即把货物交"和平"号轮装运不误。

如蒙早日办理,不胜感谢!

商祺!

John Smith 先生谨上

2. 催装运信函

敬启者:

我们想提请你方注意500匹蓝毛哔叽布的订单,订单号为5781。大约30天前我们已将开具好的该批订货的一张不可撤销信用证寄给贵方,信用证的有效期至3月31日。

由于销售旺季已快速临近,我们的客房急需这批货物。谨请你方尽快发货,以便他们在销售旺季开始时能及时满足旺盛的需求。

我们想强调一下,延误交运/发运我方订货会给我方造成极大的困难/麻烦。

对于你方的合作,预致谢意/感谢。

商祺!
XXX

Task 2　Structure of Business Letters

Preparing

✓ Relative Reading

Basic Parts of a Business English Letter

Most business letters have 7 standard parts. They are: the letterhead, the date, inside address, the salutation, the body, the complimentary close, and the signature.

Although diversity occurs in stylistic features concerning elements in business letters, writers generally agree on the standard elements of letter.

Performing

✔ Seven Principle Parts in a Business Letter

1. Letterhead（信头）

A letterhead is usually printed in advance, It represents the name and address of the sender's company, so that the receiver can know where the letter comes from and returns to it in time. It includes the essential particulars about the writer— his name, postal address and zip-code, telephone, facsimile numbers and e-mail address. Some letterheads also contain the names and titles of the person in charge of the company.

Example 1:
Richard Thomas & Baldwins Ltd.
151 Gower Street
London, SCT 6DY, England
Tel: 63216260
Fax: 63302700

Example 2:
Jameson & Sons Company Ltd.
34 Madison Square
Melbourne E. C. 2.
Australia
Tel: +61-2-70525354
Fax: +61-2-70525354

Two Functions of Letterhead
1) to identify where the letter comes from.
2) to form one's impression of the writer's company.

2. Date（日期）

It usually put one or two lines under the letterhead on the right for indented style or the left for the blocked style. Simple ways of writing are as follows.

Example:
March 16, 2018
March 16th, 2018
16 March, 2018
16th March, 2018

(1) Functions of Date

To record when the letter was written and served as important reference.

(2) Ways of Writing Date

August 3, 2012—American form

3rd August, 2012—British form

It is unwise to abbreviate the name of the month or show the date in figure like 3/8/2012.

(3) Position of Date

The date is usually placed in two lines below the last line of the letterhead, at left margin for full block style or ending with the right margin for indented style.

3. Inside Name and Address (封内地址)

It should be the same as in the envelop, which shall be the name and address of the receiver. Care should be taken that the courtesy title like "Mr." will be added before the name of the receiver.

> Example:
> Mr. Goe Smith
> General Manger
> Cowls Engineering Co. Ltd.
> 12 Braken Hill
> Manchester
> England

(1) Contents of Inside Name and Address

Name; address; zip code.

(2) Types of Inside Name and Address

1) The receiver is a company

   The Acme Shoe Co. Ltd.
   369 Piccadilly
   London
   UK

2) The receiver is an individual in a company

   Mr. Sarah Davis
   Sales Manager
   The Acme Shoe Co. Ltd.
   369 Piccadilly
   London
   UK

[注] Mr.（先生） Mrs.（夫人） Miss（小姐） Ms.（女士）

4. Salutation（称呼）

1) The salutation is the polite greeting with which the writer begins or opens his letter.

2) Dear sir, Dear Madam, Dear sirs, Dear Mesdames, Gentlemen（不能用单数）, Dear Mr. xxx.

- If the letter is addressed to an individual, it is usual to use: Dear sir, Dear Madam, Dear Mr. Smith, Dear Ms. John, Dear Prof. Hobart, Dear Dr. Walter.
- When addressing a letter to a firm, Dear Sirs, Ladies and gentlemen, Gentlemen (American English) would be used.
- The trend is towards Ms. as the courtesy title for all women regardless of their marital status.

It is the polite greeting with which a letter begins. "Dear" is used to express respect here.

Example:
Dear Sirs,
Dear Sir or Madam,
Gentlemen,

5. Body of the Letter（正文）

It is the part that the writer expresses his ideas or requirements. Usually, it is divided into three parts: opening, body and closing.

（1） Position of Body in the Letter

The body of the letter should begin two lines below the subject line, if there is one, at least two lines below the salutation if there is no subject line.

（2） Contents of Body in the Letter

1) the opening sentence — the first paragraph
2) the actual message of the letter — paragraph two, three…
3) the closing sentence — the last paragraph

The opening sentence

Thank you for your letter 25 GW of September 19th…

Your letter of the 10th, August has been received with thanks.

In reply to your letter of July 11th…

With great delight I learn that…

I have the pleasure to tell you that…

The closing sentence

We look forward to hearing from you soon.

Please do not hesitate to contract us if you require any further information.

We would be grateful if you could send us this information as soon as possible.

6. Complimentary Close (结束语)

The complimentary close is merely a polite way of ending a letter. There are many ways of complementary close to show respect. It carries no specific meanings. Usually we keep them in pace with the salutation. When the salutation is "Dear sir (s)", complimentary close will be "yours faithfully, yours sincerely"; when the salutation uses "Gentleman (men)", complimentary close will be "yours truly, truly yours", etc.

Example:

Dear Sirs,
Dear Sir,
Dear Madam,   } Yours faithfully,
Dear Sir or Madam,

Dear Mr. Black,
Dear Miss Yang,   } Yours sincerely,
Dear Jim,

Gentlemen,   —— Yours truly,

7. Signature (签名)

It is usually printed and written on a letter, the place of which will depend on the layout of the letter. We put the signature below the complimentary close. If the writer represents certain institute, the name of the institute will be printed above the signature.

Example:

THE NEW YORK TRADING COMPANY

(Signature)

Tom Smith

General Manager

1) All letters must be signed. Unsigned letter has no authority.

2) a letter should be signed by hand, in ink, and followed by the person's name typed.

eg: Yours faithfully,

The Overseas Co. Ltd.

(signature)

W. Black

President (job title or position)

✓ Six Optional Parts in a Business Letter

In a business letter, the following six parts may be chosen or not as the writer wishes.

1. Reference Number（参考号）

It is often made to the previous letter. It may include the date of the letter, a file number, the contract number or L/C number and be taken as the form as "Our ref", and "Your ref".

Example:
Your ref. S/C123

2. Attention Line（送交，具体收信人）

An "attention line" is considered as a part of the inside name and address and it leads to the letter to a particular person or department when the letter is addressed to a company.

Richard Thomas & Baldwins Ltd.
151 Gower Street
London, SC7 6DY, England
Attention Mr. Cave

or Attention of Purchasing Manager

When the writer wants to address the letter to a special person or a corporation, he will add it under the inside name and address.

Example:
Attention: The Sales Manager（由广告经理亲阅）

3. Subject Line（主题，事由）

It is a brief indication of the content of the letter. It is often inserted between the salutation and the message of the letter to invite attention to the topic of the letter.

Example:
Re.: Order No. 455
Sub.: Order No. 455

(1) **Function of Subject Line**

To help the reader obtain the gist of the letter quickly.

(2) **Position of Subject Line**

It comes with two lines below the salutation, beginning either at the left margin or in the centre, depending on which style you are using.

(3) **Content of Subject Line**

Name of commodity; quantity; number of L/C; number of S/C.

1) Re: Sewing Machines.
2) Subject: Our Contract No. 2345. Your L/C No. 345.
3) Sewing Machines.

4. Enclosure（附件）

Sometimes catalogue, price list, order or other relative documents will be enclosed in the letter, then under the signature. A line on the left will be added to remind the receiver.

Example:

Enclosure: 3 copies

Encl.: As stated

5. Carbon Copy（抄送）

It is to show that the letter has been sent to someone else which is always placed under the enclosure on the left.

Example:

Cc: The Advertising Manager

6. Postscript（附言）

It refers to something forgotten in the letter. A postscript is used as a device to draw the reader's attention to a point which the writer wants to emphasize. Don't use a postscript if you forget to mention a point in the body of the letter.

eg: P. S. I am going to see you at the Chinese Export Corporation.

Example:

P. S.: The sample will be sent to you on May 22.

 The Use of Sub-item Cases of the Parts of a Foreign Business Correspondence

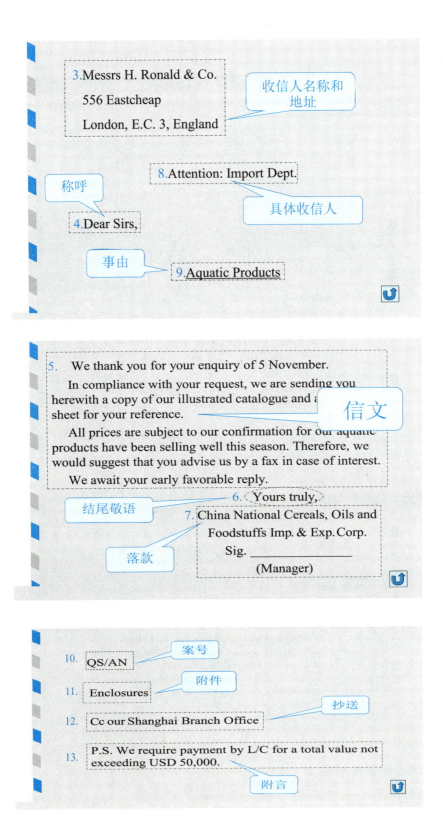

Notes

信函各部分的写法

1. 信头和收信人名称、地址

英语：名称在上，地址在下。地址先小后大。
中文：名称在上，地址在下。地址先大后小。

2. 名称、地址

3. 中国地址名称用英文写

4. 中国地名的翻译规范

用汉语拼音直译：一个地名只大写第一个字母。
例如："河南新乡"

Xinxiang, Henan ☺

Xin Xiang, He Nan ☹

可用缩写：

Rd. = Road, Fl. = Floor, Ave = Avenue.

5. 日期

位置

美式：在信头和收信人名称地址之间。

英式：通常在收信人名称地址之下。

二者均可以齐头，也可以靠右。

写法

美式：月-日-年。

英式：日-月-年。

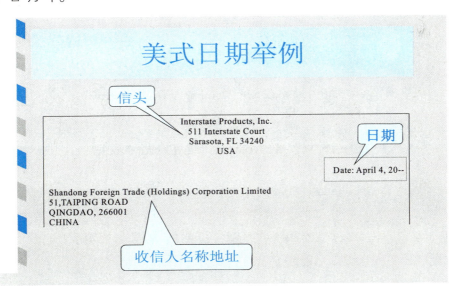

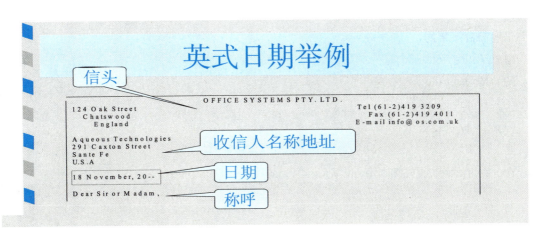

6. 日期写法注意事项

月份最好用文字，如：

(1) 2nd May, 20—

(2) 2 May, 20—

(3) September 21st, 20—

(4) September 21, 20—

(5) 25 Aug. 20—

(6) Oct. 10, 20—

7. 称呼

8. 结尾敬语

位置：

齐头式靠左对齐，缩进式偏右。

正规场合下常用：

(1) Yours faithfully,

(2) Yours truly,

(3) Faithfully yours,

(4) Truly yours,

建议使用：

Yours sincerely, 或 Sincerely yours,

9. 称呼与结尾敬语的对应关系

称呼与结尾敬语的对应关系

Salutation	Close	Occasion
Dear Sir(s) Dear Sir or Madam (Mmes)	Yours faithfully Faithfully yours	Standard and formal closure
Gentlemen Ladies/Gentlemen	Yours (very) truly Very truly yours	Used by Americans
Dear Mr. Malone	Yours sincerely/ Sincerely Best wishes (U.K.) Best regards/ Regards (U.S.)	Less formal and between persons known to each other

建议使用（指向第三行）

10. 落款

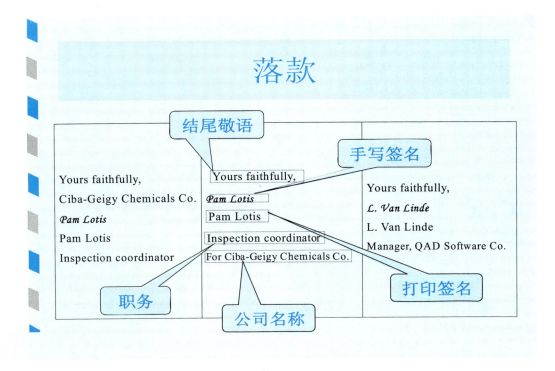

11. 具体收信人

位置：

（1）收信人名称地址之下

（2）齐头式靠左，缩进式居中

（3）要加下划线

表示的是承办本信件的具体个人或部门。

（1） Attention: Mr. H. A. Donnan, Export Manager

（2） Attention of Mr. Cave

（3） To the attention of Mr. Liu Ming

（4） ATTN: Mr. Iverson

12. 事由

位置：

（1）称呼和正文之间

（2）齐头式靠左，缩进式居中

（3）要加下划线

表示的是该信函的主题。

（1） Re: Your Order No. 463

（2） Subject: SHEEP WOOL

（3） Contract No. 8904

13. 附件

位置：

落款之下，左对齐，说明该信件有附件。

（1） Enclosure

（2） Enc.

（3） Encl. As Stated

（4） Enclosure: Brochure

14. 抄送

位置：

附件之下，左对齐，表示该信件同时抄送给他人。

（1）明抄：cc Marketing Department，(cc, Carbon copy，收信人知道被抄送)

（2）暗抄：bcc Mr. Simpson（bcc, Blind carbon copy，收信人不知道被抄送，只出现在发给被抄送人的信件里）

Situation 1　　Introductory Remarks

Practicing

I. Translate the following from English to Chinese.

letterhead	essential particular
postal address	zip-code
facsimile number	e-mail address
Inside name and address	the same as
envelop	the name and address of the receiver
courtesy	salutation
polite greeting	express respect
message	ideas or requirements
be divided into	opening, body and closing
complimentary close	mere a polite way of ending a letter
carry no specific meaning	Yours faithfully
Yours sincerely	Yours truly
signature	depend on
the layout of the letter	represent certain institute
reference number	the previous letter
date of the letter	a file number
the contract number	L/C number
take as the form as "Our ref" and "Your ref"	attention line
a special person or a corporation	the sales manager
subject line	a brief indication
inserted between the salutation and the message of the letter	
to invite attention to	the topic of the letter
enclosure	catalogue
pricelist	order
other relative documents	on the left
remind the receiver	carbon copy
under the enclosure on the left	the advertising manager
postscript	refer to

II. Translate the following Chinese business letters into English and analyze the structure of these letters.

1. 建立贸易关系信函

先生们：

　　事由：缝纫机

本公司是拉哥斯最大的缝纫机进口商之一，我们经营各种牌号的缝纫机已有20余年了。我们热切地希望与你公司建立贸易关系，发展我们两国之间贸易。随函附上第303号询价单一张，盼望你方早日给我们报拉哥斯到岸价，包括我们的佣金5%，报价时请寄目录本10份，以便我们了解你们产品的质量。倘若你方报价具有竞争性，我们打算购500台。如蒙早日复信，不胜感激。

×××谨上

2017年8月8日

2. 通知卖方已开立信用证信函

尊敬的先生们：

订单号789——自行车

我们已请洛杉矶大通银行（the Chase Bank of Los Angeles）开立一张10万美元的信用证，以贵行为受益人，有效期至5月30日。信用证将由中国银行上海分行保兑。该行将凭单承兑发票所开金额。

议付需要凭下列单证：

商业发票一式三份；

提单一式二份；

保险单一份。

自行车装运后请立即通知我们。

×××谨上

××××年×月×日

Task 3 The Process and Writing Principles of Business Letters

📝 Preparing

 Relative Reading

The Writing Techniques of Business English Letters

- Simplify the Words
- Adopt the Right Tone

- Note the Use of Jargon
- Use Active Voice rather than Passive Voice
- Vary Sentence Length
- Take Suitable Paragraph Length

In short, we not only need to be familiar with "7Cs" but also demand to learn well about some writing techniques except that we should know well about the layout of business English letters. Only in this way, we do can write an effective and attractive business English letter.

The General Procedures for Letter writing

How shall we deal with business letter writing? Generally, the writing process consists of the following five steps. While writing, ask yourself the relevant questions following each step:

a. Determine your purpose of writing: why shall I write?
b. Analyze your reader: what do I know about the receiver? What kind of relationship do we have?
c. Organize your thoughts: what shall I say? How shall I say?
d. Write your drafts: is this the best way to say what I want to say?
e. Polish your writing: is this a really effective business letter?

Performing

The Process of Writing

1) Clarifying Aim
2) Identifying Readers
3) Making a General Plan
4) Sketching a Synopsis
5) Drafting Text
6) Putting the Draft Aside
7) Revising and Editing

Writing Principles

Usually we use "7Cs" to indicate the requirements for business letter writing. About "7Cs", they are completeness, concreteness, correctness, clarity, conciseness, courtesy and consideration.

1. Completeness (完整)

A successful business letter must contain all the necessary information to the readers and answer all the questions and requirements put forward by the readers. Incompleteness will lead to the counterpart's unfavorable impression toward your firm.

In order to verify the completeness of what you write, five "Ws" and one "H" should be used.

    Who   What   When   Where   Why   How

> **Summary**
>
> (1) **Use Complete Modifier**
>
>   1) The auditorium will seat approximately 1,000 people.
>
>   2) The auditorium will seat 986 people.
>
>   3) I need the printout as soon as possible.
>
>   4) I need the printout by 3 p.m. today.
>
> (2) **Avoid Opinions or Generalizations**
>
>   1) These brakes can stop a car within a short distance.
>
>   2) These LG Brakes can stop a 2-ton car within 24 feet.
>
>   3) Our printer is faster than the leading competitor's model.
>
>   4) Our model T3 printer operates at a speed of 4,300 lines per minute.

2. Concreteness (具体)

Writing concretely means making your message specific, definite and vivid rather than vague, general and abstract. A business letter should avoid emptiness in contents and vagueness in ideas.

> **Compare**
>
> 1) We wish to confirm our fax sent yesterday.
>
> 2) We confirm our fax of October 19, 2010.
>
> The guidelines below may help you achieve concreteness:
>
> 1) Use specific facts and figures.
>
> 2) Put action in your verbs. Prefer active verbs to passive verbs or words in which action is hidden.
>
> 3) Choose vivid, concrete and image-building words.

3. Correctness (正确)

Correctness means not only proper expressions with correct grammar, punctuation and spelling, but also appropriate tone which is a help to achieve the purpose.

Business letters must have factual information, accurate figures and exact terms in particular, for they involve the right, the duties and the interest of both sides. It's the base of all kinds of documents.

Therefore we should not understate nor overstate as understatement might lead to less confidence and hold up the trade development. While overstatement throws you into an awkward position.

Example:

(1) **You Shouldn't Say**

This product is absolutely the best one on the market.

It is the lowest price available to you.

We assure you that this error will never occur.

(2) **You Should Say**

This product is the best one we can supply.

It is the lowest price we can offer now.

We will do all we can so that we may avoid such an error.

Summary

(1) **Verifying Spelling**

(2) **Select Correct Words or Phrases**

1) Anyone can learn to type.

2) Any one of us can learn to type.

3) Everyone is practicing shopping.

4) Every one of us is practicing shopping.

(3) **Insert Appropriate Punctuation.**

1) "The director", says the boss, "will have the session records".

2) The director says the boss will have the session records.

(4) The Formality of Language: (In)Formal

Formal:	Informal:
Anticipate	Expect
Ascertain	Find out
Conflagration	Fire
Endeavor	Try
Interrogate	Ask
Procure	Get

(5) Right Approaches: (In)Direct

Direct approach:

(The main ideas) —— positive message

Indirect approach:

(The main ideas)

negative message

Compare

1) It is the lowest price available to you.

2) It is the lowest price we can offer to you.

4. Clarity (清楚)

Clarity is to make sure that the words you write is so clear that it can't be misunderstood.

(1) Pay More Attention to Choosing the Concise and Accessible Expressions and Trying to Avoid the Words and Sentences Equivocal Meaning

Example:

As to the steamers sailing from Hong Kong to San Francisco, we have bimonthly direct services.

1) We have two direct sailings every month from Hong Kong to San Francisco.

2) We have direct sailing every two months from Hong Kong to San Francisco.

(2) Pay More Attention to the Position of the Modifier

The same modifier will lead to different implication and function when it is put in different position of the sentence.

Example:

1) We shall be able to supply 10 cases of the item only.

Only modify the item

2) We shall be able to supply only 10 cases of the item.

Only modify 10 cases

(3) **Pay More Attention to the Logicality of the Full Text**

Example:

1) We sent you 5 samples of the goods which you requested in your letter of May 20 by air.

2) We sent you, by air, 5 samples of the goods which you requested in your letter of May 20.

> **Summary**
>
> (1) **Use simple, Short Words and Simple Sentence Structure**
>
> after/subsequent; large/substantial
>
> use/utilize; during/in the course of;
>
> (2) **Avoid Using Words with Different Meanings**
>
> 1) We shall take a firm line with the firm.
>
> 2) We shall take a strong line with the firm.
>
> (3) **Put Words Together with Close Relation**
>
> 1) The L/C must reach us not later than 8 October for arranging shipment.
>
> 2) The L/C must reach us for arranging shipment not later than 8 October.
>
> 3) They bought a bicycle in Beijing in a small shop which costs USD 25.
>
> 4) They bought a bicycle for USD 25 in a small shop in Beijing.
>
> 5) He was warned not to drink water even in a restaurant which had not been boiled.
>
> 6) He was warned not to drink water which had not been boiled even in a restaurant.
>
> (4) **Use Active Voice**
>
> 1) A telex was sent by us yesterday.
>
> 2) We sent you a telex yesterday.
>
> 3) The application was completed by the student.
>
> 4) The student completed the application.
>
> 5) The salary increase was received by all employees.

> 6) All employees received the salary increase.
>
> **(5) Use Facts, Examples, and Visual Aids**
>
> 1) These breaks stop a car within a short distance.
> 2) These breaks stop a 2-ton car, traveling 60 miles an hour, within 240 feet.
> 3) This computer reproduces campaign letters fast.
> 4) This computer types 1,000 personalized 150-word campaign letters in one hour.

It is wise for a writer to make himself understood well by using clear expressions and simple words. He should try to avoid using the words which have unclear meanings. And the writer should also paragraph a letter carefully and properly.

> **Compare**
>
> 1) In case of sailing from Hong Kong to Osaka, we have bimonthly direct services.
> 2) We have two direct sailing every month from Hong Kong to Osaka.

5. Conciseness(简洁)

Conciseness means complete message but briefest expression with no sacrificing clarity or courtesy. A good business letter should be precise and to the point.

(1) Avoid Wordiness

enclosed here with ⟶ enclosed

at this time ⟶ now

due to the fact that ⟶ because

a draft in the amount of USD 1,000 ⟶ a draft for USD 1,000

in the event that ⟶ if

in the matter of ⟶ about

(2) Avoid Unusual Words and Out-of-Date Commercial Jargon, Try to Express Your Idea in Modern English

deem ⟶ think   take into consideration ⟶ consider

ult. ⟶ last month   utilize ⟶ use

this is to inform you of... ⟶ we are pleased to tell you

(3) Avoid Unnecessary Repeat

Example:

We have begun to export our machines to the foreign countries.

We have begun to export our machines.

(4) Control the Number of the Words, and Build Effective Sentences and Paragraphs.

Generally speaking, the average length for sentences should be 10 to 20 words, not over 30 ones.

> **Summary**
>
> **(1) Shorten Wordy Expressions**
>
> 1) We have begun to export our machines to countries abroad.
> 2) We have begun to export our machines.
> 3) For the amount of USD 320 you can buy the motor.
> 4) For USD 320 you can buy the motor.
> 5) You have won due to the fact that you arrived early.
> 6) You have won because you arrived early.
>
> **(2) Use Words to Replace Phrases or Clauses**
>
> 1) We require furniture which is of the new type.
> 2) We require new-type furniture.
> 3) For your information we enclose a catalogue.
> 4) We enclose a catalogue.
> 5) In the event that you speak to Mr. Mood in regard to the production, ask him to give consideration to the delivery order.
> 6) If you speak to Mr. Mood about the production, ask him to consider the delivery order.

A concise communication can save time and costs for both writers and readers, so the writer is required to avoid using wordy expressions or unnecessary repetition. It is needed to use short sentences, simple words and clear explanations.

> **Compare**
>
> 1) We have your remittance of May 12 in the amount of USD 1,000, and with at this time to offer our thanks to you for it.
> 2) Thank you for your remittance of May 12 for USD 1,000.

6. Courtesy (礼貌)

Courtesy means to show tactfully in your letters the honest friendship, thoughtful appreciation, sincere politeness, considerate understanding and heartfelt respect. Answer letters in good time and write to explain why if you fail to do it promptly.

Example:

1) We are sorry that you misunderstood us.

2) We are sorry that we didn't make ourselves clear.

Please Change Tone of Sentences

1) Tell me more detailed information on your requirements.

Will you tell us more detailed information on your requirements?

Would you tell us more detailed information on your requirements?

2) We cannot deliver the goods all at one time.

I'm afraid we cannot deliver the goods all at one time.

3) You ought to have accepted the offer.

It seems to us that you ought to have accepted the offer.

Summary

(1) Say Thanks, Please, Sorry

(2) Use Positive Words and Expression instead of Negative Ones

1) The office is closed after 4.

2) The office is open until 4.

3) We cannot have these figures for you before next week.

4) We will have these figures for you next week.

5) We have found out that your delinquency with regard to your account by USD 3.

6) We noticed that your account is short by USD 3.

(3) Write Naturally and Sincerely

1) I have pleasure informing you.

2) I am pleased to tell you.

3) Please be good enough to advise us.

4) Please tell us.

(4) Use "You Approach"

1) I think your report was well done.

2) Your report was well done.

3) We will accept bids until June 10.

4) You may submit a bid until June 10.

> **Compare**
>
> 1) You ought to have accepted the offer.
>
> 2) It seems to us that you ought to have accepted the offer.

7. Consideration（体谅）

Try to put yourself in his or her place to give consideration to his or her wishes, demands, interests and difficulties.

Example:

（1）**Sometimes It Is a Help to Use You-Attitude instead of I-Attitude**

A: We allow 2 percent discount for cash payment. We won't be able to send you the brochure this month.

B: You earn 2 percent discount when you pay cash. We will send you the brochure next month.

（2）**Try to Discuss Problems in a Positive Way and Avoid Discussing Problems in a Negative Way**

A: We close at 5 p.m.

B: We are open till 5 p.m.

A: We have received your complaint about the late arrival of …

B: Thank you for calling our attention to the late arrival of …

> **Summary**
>
> （1）**Establish Good Interpersonal Relations**
>
> - Put yourself in the readers' position.
> - Place the reader in the center of things.
> - Use You-attitude instead of We-attitude.
>
> 1) I want to send my congratulations …
>
> 2) Congratulations to you on your …
>
> 3) We must receive your receipt with the merchandise before we can process your refund.
>
> 4) Please enclose the sales receipt with the merchandise, so that we can process your refund promptly.
>
> （2）**Declining or Complaining in Tactful Way**
>
> 1) Apparently you have forgotten what I wrote to you two weeks ago.

> 2) As mentioned in my letter to you on May 8…
>
> 3) Your letter is not clear at all. I can't understand it.
>
> 4) If I understand your letter correctly …

An effective business writing is on the basis of putting yourself into your reader's shoes. Consideration emphasizes You-attitude rather than We-attitude. When writing a letter, keep the reader's request, needs, desires as well as his feelings in mind. Plan the best way to present the message for the reader to receive.

> **Compare**
>
> 1) We allow a 2% discount for cash payment.
>
> 2) You could earn a 2% discount for cash payment.

Practicing

I. Translate the following from English to Chinese.

writing principles	a practical business letter writing
completeness	indicate the requirements for business letter writing
successful and effective	all the necessary information
all the questions and requirements	put forward by the readers
concreteness	a business letter
specific	definite
instead of	vague
general	abstract
compare	confirm our fax
correctness	correct usage
grammar	punctuation and spelling
standard language	proper statement
accurate figures	as well as
the correct understanding	commercial jargons
the lowest price	available to
offer to	clarity
make himself understood well	using clear expressions and simple words
try to	have different understanding
unclear meaning	paragraph a letter carefully and properly

in case of sailing from Hong Kong to Osaka

We have two direct sailing every month from Hong Kong to Osaka.

conciseness   concise communication

save time and costs for both writers and readers

so the writer is required to avoid using wordy expressions or unnecessary repetition

short sentences   simple words

clear explanations   direct services

Thank you for your remittance of May 12 for USD 1,000.

polite expressions and sentences in your writing

In order to make a business letter courteous, try to avoid irritating, offensive or belittling statements.

to answer letters promptly is also a matter of courtesy

An effective business writing is on the basis of putting yourself into your reader's shoes.

Consideration emphasizes You-attitude rather than We-attitude.

keep the reader's request, needs, desires as well as his feelings in mind

Plan the best way to present the message for the reader to receive.

We allow a 2% discount for cash payment.

You could earn a 2% discount for cash payment.

II. Translate the following from English to Chinese and then answer some questions.

1. Credit Survey Letter with Attachment (带附表的资信调查函)

Dear Sir or Madam,

  We have received a sudden order from the Delta Company, Ltd., 1258 Huston Avenue, New York, NY 10051, who gives us your name as a reference.

  We shall appreciate it if you will spend a couple of minutes informing us of your own experiences with the firm by answering the attached questionnaire and returning it to us in the enclosed envelope.

  Any information you may give us will be treated as strictly confidential. Thank you for your help.

Very truly yours,
Thomas

Attached Questions

  a. How long have you been in business relations with the firm?

    …years? …months?

  b. What credit limit have you placed on their account?

c. How promptly are terms met? (choose one of the following)
   Very promptly   Fairly promptly   Slowly
d. What amount is currently outstanding?
   USD

2. Resume Relation with Old Customers (与过去有贸易往来的公司恢复联系)

Dear Thomas Moore,

We understand from our trade contacts that your company has reestablished itself and is once again trading successfully in your region. We would like to extend our congratulations and offer our very best wishes for your continued success. In the past, our companies were involved in a large volume of trade in our textiles. We see from our records that you were among our best long-term customers. We hope very much that we can resume our mutually beneficial relationship now. Since we last traded, our lines have changed beyond recognition. While they reflect current European taste in fabrics, some of our designs are specifically targeted at the Middle Eastern market. As an initial step, I enclose our illustrated catalogue for your perusal. Should you wish to receive samples for closer inspection, we will be very happy to forward them. We look forward to hearing from you.

Yours sincerely,
David Parker

Attached Questions

a. Why did the writer wrote this letter?
b. The companies were involved in a large volume of trade in our textiles, right or wrong?
c. What would the writer like to extend and offer?
d. Should you wish to receive samples for closer inspection?
e. Please describe the main idea of this letter.

Situation 02: Establishing Business Relations

📝 Objectives

1) To be able to translate and write a letter of establishing business relations properly.
2) To be able to translate and write reply to business relations establishment letter.

📝 Introduction

No customer, no business. Establishing business relations with prospective dealers is the base of starting and developing business. It is important for a new dealer and an old one. If a firm wishes to open up a new market to sell or buy something from foreign countries, the person in charge must first of all find out whom he is going to deal with. Usually, the following channels are available:

1) Communicating in writing
2) Attending the export commodities fairs
3) Holding exhibitions home and abroad
4) Visiting trade delegations and groups

Of all the above channels, the first one is widely used in business activities.

· Main Points of Establishing Business Relations

1) Stating the source of customer's information
2) Introducing briefly one's own company
3) Expressing the purpose of writing the letter
4) Expressing the wish of business relations establishment and early reply

· Main Points of Replies

1) Thanking for the coming letter

2) a. Expressing willingness of business relations establishment and making a brief self-introduction.

　　b. Regretting for the inability to establish business relations and state the reason.

3) a. Hoping for conducting business activities.

　　b. Expressing the expectation of cooperation in the future.

Task 1　The First Communication from the Seller

Preparing

✓ Relative Reading

What are Exports?

Exports are defined as movable goods produced within the boundaries of one country, which are traded with another country. The sale of these goods generates foreign currency earnings in the country that produces them and boosts its economic growth. The greater the proportion of exports in relation to a country's Gross Domestic Product (GDP), the larger the boost will be to overall growth when overseas demand increases. Demand for exports is subject to economic conditions in foreign countries as well as prices, quality perception and reliability. In addition, a country's production and flow of exports depend on trade restrictions, such as tariffs, quotas and subsidies, both domestically and abroad.

✓ Lead In — Dialogues

Xu Wei (A) and John Brown (B) are at the fair.

A: Excuse me, can I help you?

B: Yes, I'd like to see some printers.

A: This way, please. We'll be glad to show you what's available. Here's my card. I'm Xu Wei from Kaiyue Co. Ltd. and our company mainly manufactures varieties of printers.

B: Thanks. Mr. Xu. Here's my card.

A: Thank you. Please have a look at our samples.

B: Your products seem remarkable.

A: Most of our products are color laser jet with various other functions to meet the needs of different customers.

Situation 2   Establishing Business Relations

B: I see.

A: So is there any item that you are interested in?

B: I think I've already seen some items we might like to order, although I'd still like to study them a bit further.

A: OK, go ahead.

B: I'll probably be able to let you know tomorrow.

A: I'll be expecting you tomorrow morning, say, at nine.

B: Tomorrow at nine. Good. I'll see you then.

Performing

Text

Sample 1   Exporter's Self-Introduction

Dear Sir or Madam,

We have obtained your name and address from the Commercial Counselor's Office of British Embassy in Beijing.

We are one of the largest printer manufacturers in our country and have handled the line for more than 20 years. We can assure you of our products' fine quality with competitive prices.

Enclosed please find a copy of our catalog for your reference and hope you could contact us if any item is of interest to you.

Looking forward to your favorable reply ASAP.

Yours sincerely,
Zhu Kai
ABC Co. Ltd.

Sample 2   Reply to the Above

Dear Sir,

Thank you for your letter of May 18.

We are one of the largest importers of office supplies in our city and glad to establish business relations with your company.

At present, we are interested in your printer MP 258 in the catalog you sent us.

We look forward to receiving your best quotation.

Yours sincerely,
Mike Smith

Sample 3　Establishment of Business Relations

Dear Sirs,

　　We have obtained your address from the Commercial Counselor of your Embassy in London and are now writing you for the establishment of business relations.

　　We are very well connected with all the major dealers here of light industrial products, and feel sure that we can sell large quantities of Chinese goods if we get your offers at competitive prices.

　　As to our standing, we are permitted to mention the Bank of England, London, as a reference.

　　Please let us have all necessary information regarding your products for export.

Yours faithfully,

Notes

1) obtain ... from ...　从哪里获悉……
   类似的表达还有 "from..., we learn that..." "be glad/pleased to know that..."

2) Commercial Counselor's Office of British Embassy in Beijing
   英国驻华大使馆商务参赞处

3) handle　v. deal with, trade in　经营
   e. g. We don't handle that sort of book. 我们不经销那一类书。

4) line　n. business scope　行业，生意范围
   be in the line of ...　在……范围之内
   deal with/ handle the line of ...　在……处理线上

5) assure sb. of sth.; assure sb. that ...　向某人确保某物或某事

6) fine quality with competitive prices　价廉物美

7) Enclosed please find ...　随函附上……
   e. g. Enclosed please find our price list and samples. 随函附上我方价目表及样品。

8) establish business relations with　建立贸易关系
   类似的表达还有：set up/ build up/ enter into business relations with sb.
   n. establishment
   establishment of business relations　建立业务关系
   establishment of L/C　开立信用证

9) sth. be of interest to sb.　某物使某人感兴趣
   sb. be interested in sth. /doing sth.　某人对某物或对做某事感兴趣
   sth. be interesting to sb.　某人对某事很感兴趣

10）look forward to + sth. /doing sth.　期待……
11）ASAP　"as soon as possible"的缩写，常用商务用语
12）office supplies　办公用品
13）quotation　报价

Practicing

I. Translate the following expressions into English.

有限公司　　　　　　　建立业务关系
产品目录　　　　　　　在……行业
商务参赞处　　　　　　品质优良
以供参考　　　　　　　有竞争力的价格
经营　　　　　　　　　最低报价

II. Choose the best answer to complete each of the following sentences.

1. We are sending you the samples _____ requested.
    A. be   B. are   C. as   D. for
2. We trust that you will find our goods _____.
    A. attracting   B. to be attractive
    C. attract your attention   D. attractive
3. We look forward _____ your favorable news.
    A. on   B. to   C. at   D. of
4. Thank you for the sample _____ in your letter.
    A. enclose   B. being enclosed   C. enclosing   D. enclosed
5. We take the pleasure of introducing ourselves _____ a leading importer _____ of daily products.
    A. of, on   B. as, in   C. for, by   D. be, at
6. We will forward all necessary information _____ receipt of your reply.
    A. with   B. in   C. upon   D. of
7. _____ in 2005, this company specializes in the export of cotton piece goods.
    A. Established   B. Establish
    C. Establishing   D. To be established
8. _____ create severe competition for home produced goods.
    A. Import   B. Importing   C. Imports   D. Imported
9. We wish to build up business relations _____ you.
    A. on   B. of   C. in   D. with

10. We are writing to you _____ you can give us the lowest quotation.
    A. hope   B. hoping to   C. in the hope to   D. in the hope that

III. Translate the following sentences into Chinese.

1. We write to you today in the hope of establishing business relations with you.
2. If you are interested in any item listed in our catalogue, please let us know ASAP.
3. We would like to enter into direct business relations with you on the basis of equality and mutual benefit.
4. We specialize in the export business of light industrial products for more than thirty years.
5. We thank you for your letter of June 12 and should like to discuss the possibility of expanding trade between us.

IV. Writing practice.

1. Write a letter stating the following points.
   1) You are introduced by the Commercial Counselor's Office of their embassy in Beijing.
   2) You wish to set up business relations with them.
   3) The main scope of our business is exporting chinaware.
   4) Samples and catalogues will be sent to them upon receipt of their specific enquiries.
2. Write a letter about establishing business relations.

Supplement

✓ Supplementary Reading

1. Letter: An Unfavorable Reply

Dear Mr. Zhu,

We have received your letter with thanks on May 7, 2010. We, however, regret to inform you that we are not in a position to enter into business relations with you because we have already been appointed as an agent by Guangdong Trade Corporation for the sale of their products.

Under the circumstances, we regret to say that we can't transact with you at least until the agency contract expires. Of course, we filed your letter and catalogue for our future reference. So we may contact you when we become free from the agency contract.

We thank you again and hope you will understand our situation fully.

Yours faithfully,
Jenny Brown

2. Reading: Levels of Relationship Marketing

What type of relationships should an organization have with its customers? Is the cost of keeping a relationship worth it? To answer these questions, let's define the three general levels of selling relationships with customers:

Transaction selling: customers are sold to and not contacted again.

Relationship selling: the seller contacts to improve its customers' operations, sales, and profits.

Most organizations focus solely on the single transaction with each customer. When you go to McDonald's and buy a hamburger, that's it. You never hear from them again unless you return for another purchase. The same thing happens when you go to a movie, rent a video, open a bank checking account, visit the grocery store, or have your clothes cleaned. Each of these examples involves low-priced, low-profit products. Also involved are a large number of customers who are geographically dispersed. This makes it very difficult and quite costly to contact customers. The business is forced to use transactional marketing.

The seller contacts the customer to ensure satisfaction with the purchase. The Cadillac Division of General Motors contacts each buyer of a new Cadillac to determine the customer's satisfaction with the car. If that person is not satisfied, General Motors works with the retailer selling the car to make sure the customer is happy.

Partnering is a phenomenon of the 1990s, businesses' growing concern over the competition not only in America but also internationally revitalized their needs to work closely with important customers. The familiar 80/20 principle states that 80 percent of sales often come from 20 percent of a company's customers. Organizations now realize the need to identify their most important customers and designate them for their partnering programs. The organization's best salespeople are assigned to sell and service these customers. Let's take a closer look at partnering since it is becoming so important to organizations.

✔ Knowledge Link

☆ 大使馆

大使馆是一国在建交国首都派驻的常设外交代表机构。

大使馆的首要职责是代表派遣国促进两国的政治关系，其次是促进经济、文化、教育和科技等方面的关系。

大使馆的职责范围遍及所驻国的各个地区，而领事馆只负责所辖地区。大使馆通常受政府和外交部门的直接领导，而领事馆则通常接受外交部门和所驻国大使馆的双重领导。在一个国家里，大使馆只有一个，而领事馆可以在很多城市都有。

☆ 商务参赞

参赞是外交官的一种职衔，其外交地位仅次于大使、公使。参赞的主要任务是协助使馆馆长进行工作，使馆馆长因故缺位时，通常由作为首席馆员的政务参赞担任临时代办，代为主持馆务。参赞分为公使衔参赞、政务参赞、商务参赞、经济参赞、文化参赞和教育参赞等。各国在其使馆中设置哪些参赞，根据其情况与需要而定。使馆通常设有商务参赞和文化参赞。

商务参赞是使馆中负责同驻在国外贸部门进行联系和交涉的外交人员，一般由派遣国外贸主管部门派出。其职责是向本国主管部门报告驻在国的经济和贸易发展情况，准备贸易协定的签订工作并监督其执行，签订或协作签订重要的贸易合同。商务参赞通常是使馆商务处负责人，享有外交特权和豁免。

Task 2 The First Communication from the Buyer

Preparing

Relative Reading

What are Imports?

The quantity or value of all that is imported into a country. "Imports" consist of transactions in goods and services to a resident of a jurisdiction (such as a nation) from non-residents. The exact definition of imports in national accounts includes and excludes specific "borderline" cases. Importation is the action of buying or acquiring products or services from another country or another market. Imports are important for the economy because they allow a country to supply nonexistent, scarce, high cost or low quality of certain products or services, to its market with products from other countries.

A general delimitation of imports in national accounts is given below:

An import of a good occurs when there is a change of ownership from a non-resident to a resident; this does not necessarily imply that the good in question physically crosses the frontier. However, in specific cases national accounts impute changes of ownership even though in legal terms no change of ownership takes place (e.g. cross border financial leasing, cross border deliveries between affiliates of the same enterprise, goods crossing the border for significant processing to order or repair). Also smuggled goods must be included in the import measurement.

Situation 2　Establishing Business Relations

Imports of services consist of all services rendered by non-residents to residents. In national accounts any direct purchases by residents outside the economic territory of a country are recorded as imports of services; therefore all expenditure by tourists in the economic territory of another country are considered part of the imports of services. Also international flows of illegal services must be included.

Basic trade statistics often differ in terms of definition and coverage from the requirements in the national accounts.

✔ Lead In — Dialogues

Wang Ning (A) from Blue Sky Mold Company and her potential customer Martin Jones (B) are having a phone conversation.

A: Hello! This is Wang Ning, marketing assistant of TA Mold.
B: Hello, Miss Wang. This is Martin Jones from Leigh Mardon Company. I'm interested in your plastic mold. I've seen some samples in Canton Fair. They are very impressive.
A: Thank you for your interest in our products. They are high quality products and have been exported to more than 40 countries and areas with high identification.
B: I see. And could you give me a brief introduction of your products?
A: Okay, Mr. Jones. But you know, for each model, we have a series of products. May I fax you a catalogue?
B: No, you needn't. I have got one copy. I'm really interested in the prices of your products.
A: In that case, I think we do need a talk.
B: That's exactly what I'm thinking! When will it be convenient for you?
A: It is up to you. But I hope you can come to visit our company.
B: I'll fly to Ningbo next Monday morning. Is that alright for you?
A: That's great! I will meet you at the airport.
B: Thank you. I will email you the flight number. See you then.
A: See you.

❖ Performing

✔

Sample 1　Importer's Self-Introduction

Dear Sir or Madam,

　　We have learnt your name and address from the internet, and we are writing to you in the hope of establishing business relations with you.

We are one of the largest importers of fresh fruits and vegetables in Zhejiang, China and have enjoyed a good reputation through decades of business experience.

We are now interested in your green farm produces and will appreciate your catalogs and price lists very much? If your prices are competitive, we would like to place a trial order with you.

We look forward to receiving your early reply.

Yours sincerely,

Sample 2   Reply to the Above

Dear Sir,

Thank you for your letter of January 8.

We are one of the largest exporters of green farm produces in our city and glad to set up business relations with your company.

As requested, we enclose our catalog covering the main items supplied now and our latest price list for your reference. Please rest assured that our products are excellent in quality and reasonable in price.

We are looking forward to your specific enquiries.

Yours sincerely,

Sample 3   An Introduction of an Importer

Dear Sir,

We have obtained your address in *China Daily* and are now writing to you for the establishment of business relations.

We are very well connected with all suppliers of agricultural products. Now, we are very interested in your beans and wheat. We feel sure that we can sell large quantities of them if we get your offers with competitive prices.

For our credit standing, please refer to the following bank:

The Bank of Australia and New Zealand, Australia.

Your immediate reply would be highly appreciated.

Yours faithfully,
(Signature)
Amy Harry

Situation 2 Establishing Business Relations

Notes

1) in the hope of 希望

   in the hope of sth. / doing sth. / that... 怀着……的希望，抱着……的希望

2) reputation 好名声，声誉

   enjoy/have a (high) reputation 享有佳誉

   e. g. This store has an excellent reputation for fair dealing.
   这家商店因公平交易而获好名声。

3) green farm produces 绿色农产品

4) appreciate v. be thankful or show gratitude for 感谢，欣赏

   We shall appreciate it if... 假如……，我方将不胜感激

   It is appreciated if/that... 假如……，我方将不胜感激

   We shall appreciate you doing... 我们将感谢您所做的……；您所做的……，我们将不胜感激

   We shall appreciate sth. 我们将感激某事

5) competitive adj. 有竞争力的，竞争的

   competitive price 有竞争力的价格

6) order n. 订单

   trial order 试订单

   repeat order 续订单

   substantial order 大宗订单

   first order 首次订单

   place an order with sb. for sth. 向某人订购……

7) our products are excellent in quality and reasonable in price 我们的产品价廉物美

8) enquiry n. 询问，打听，询盘

   make an enquiry/ enquiries 询盘

   enquire v. 询问，打听，询盘

   enquire for sth. 询盘某种商品

   enquire about sth. 打听某事

   enquire into sth. 调查某事

Practicing

I. Translate the following expressions into Chinese.

largest importer   enjoy a good reputation

decades of business experience price list

as requested	trial order
rest assured	specific enquiry
enquire into sth.	substantial order

II. Fill in the blanks with proper forms of given words.

> appreciate   compete   enquire   establish   desire

1. Upon receipt of your specific _____, we'll send you the quotation.
2. Your price is _____ and acceptable to us.
3. We're writing for the _____ of business relations with your company.
4. We have a _____ to buy this product from you.
5. We would _____ it very much if you send us a few sample books.

III. Translate the following sentences into English.

1. 我们向贵方保证我们的产品质优价廉。
2. 从贵方6月5日的来函获悉贵方打算购买我方的丝绸产品。
3. 本公司是本地一家中等规模的玩具出口商，在欧美市场享有佳誉。
4. 期待早日收到贵方的答复。
5. 如果你方价格有竞争力，我们相信我们之间能达成大量的交易。

IV. Writing practice.

You are a large French importer of cotton piece goods and you got a piece of information about leading manufacturer of the line in Asia. You are interested in their products. Now write a letter to them hoping to establish business relations with them.

Supplement

Supplementary Reading

1. Letter 1: Building the Trade Relations

Dear Sir,

We saw your Fat-reducing Tea at the International Exhibition of National Health Products held in Italy during October, and are keenly interested in this product.

With a view to building the trade relations with you, we are writing to you and hope to receive your catalogues and price lists for reference.

As one of the leading American importers of health products, we are experiencing in pushing sales of the products and have good connections with wholesalers and retailers in the country. If your prices are in line, we trust important business can materialize.

Situation 2 Establishing Business Relations

We anticipate your early reply.

Yours faithfully,

2. Letter 2: Reply to the Above

Dear sirs,

We learned about you at the China Import and Export Fair.

Being one of the largest importers of Chinese Arts & Crafts in this city, we shall be pleased to establish business relations with you.

At present, we are interested in your products, details as per our Inquiry Note No. 618 attached, and shall be glad to receive your keenest quotation as soon as possible.

Yours,

3. Reading

In international trade, the importer is usually in one country while the exporter is in another country. They are separated sometimes by thousands of miles. Establishing the business relations is the first step in the transaction in foreign trade.

Writing letters to new customers for establishment of relations is a common practice in business communications. To establish the business relations with prospective dealers is one of the vitally important measures either for a newly established firm or an old one that wished to enlarge its business scope and turnover. There are several channels through which imports and exporters can get to know each other. Generally speaking, this type of letter begins by telling the address how his or her name is known. The writer should state simply, clearly and concisely what he can sell or what he expects to buy.

Any letter of this nature received must be answered in full without the least delay and with courtesy so as to create goodwill and leave a good impression on the reader. The first impression counts heavily. Make sure that your letters follows the standard format and that it is neatly typed and error-free. To firms engaged in foreign trade, the business connections are valuable. Therefore, traders must not only do everything possible to consolidate their established relations with firms having previous business but also develop and revitalize their trade by searching for new connections from time to time.

✓ **Knowledge Link**

☆ 广交会

广交会，全称为中国进出口商品交易会，创办于1957年春季，每年春秋两季在广州举办，迄今已有六十余年历史，是中国目前历史最长、层次最高、规模最大、商品种类最全、到会客商最多、成交效果最好的综合性国际贸易盛会，被誉为"中国第一展"。自2007年4月第101届起，广交会由中国出口商品交易会更名为中国进出口商品交易会，由单一出口平台变为进出口双向交易平台。

中国进出口商品交易会贸易方式灵活多样，除传统的看样成交外，还举办网上交易会。广交会以出口贸易为主，也做进口生意，还可以开展多种形式的经济技术合作与交流，以及商检、保险、运输、广告和咨询等业务活动。

☆ 阿里巴巴网站

阿里巴巴（www. alibaba. com）是全球企业间（B2B）电子商务的著名品牌，是目前全球最大的网上交易市场和商务交流社区，被商人们评为"最受欢迎的B2B网站"。

阿里巴巴曾入选哈佛大学商学院MBA案例，在美国学术界掀起研究热潮；两次被美国权威财经杂志《福布斯》选为全球最佳B2B站点之一；多次被相关机构评为全球最受欢迎的B2B网站、中国商务类优秀网站、中国百家优秀网站和中国最佳贸易网等。

阿里巴巴创始人、阿里巴巴集团董事局主席马云被著名的"世界经济论坛"选为"未来领袖"，被美国亚洲商业协会选为"商业领袖"，是50多年来第一位成为《福布斯》封面人物的中国企业家，并曾多次应邀为全球著名高等学府麻省理工学院、沃顿商学院、哈佛大学讲学。阿里巴巴成立至今，全球十几种语言400多家著名新闻传媒对阿里巴巴的追踪报道从未间断，被传媒界誉为"真正的世界级品牌"。

Task 3　Credit Inquiry

Preparing

Relative Reading

What is Credit Inquiry?

A credit inquiry is a request by an institution for credit report information from a credit reporting agency. Credit inquiries can be from all types of entities for various reasons. They are classified as either a hard inquiry or a soft inquiry.

Breaking down "Credit Inquiry"

Credit inquiries are a significant component of the credit market. Hard inquiries are a key part of the underwriting process for all types of credit. Soft inquiries help credit companies to market their products and can also be used to help consumers.

Hard Inquiries

Hard inquiries are requested from a credit bureau whenever a borrower completes a new credit application. They are retrieved by a customer's social security number and are required for the credit underwriting process. Hard inquiries provide a creditor with a full credit report on a borrower. This report will include a borrower's credit score as well as details on their credit history.

Hard inquiries can be harmful to a borrower's credit score. Each hard inquiry usually causes a small credit score decrease for a borrower. Hard inquiries remain on one's credit report for two years. Generally a high number of hard credit inquiries in a short period of time can be interpreted as an attempt to substantially expand available credit which creates higher risks for a lender.

In some instances hard inquiries may also be used for situations other than a credit application. An employment background check and a lease rental application are two instances when a hard inquiry may also be required.

Soft Inquiries

Soft inquiries are not included on a credit report. These inquiries can be requested for a variety of reasons. Credit companies have relationships with credit bureaus for soft inquiries that result in marketing lists for potential customers. These soft inquiries are customized by the credit company to identity borrowers that meet some of their underwriting characteristics for a loan. Credit aggregating services also use soft inquiries to help borrowers find a loan. These platforms require information about a borrower including their social security number which allows for soft inquiries and prequalification offers. Many lenders will also provide a borrower with quotes through a soft inquiry request that can help them understand potential loan terms.

Personal credit reports are also obtained through soft inquiries. Individuals have a right to obtain free annual credit reports from credit reporting agencies that detail their credit information. Individuals can also sign up for free credit scores through their credit card companies. These credit scores are reported to borrowers each month and are obtained by the credit card company through a soft inquiry.

Background Information of Credit Inquiry

Importance of Credit Inquiry

Before you start to do business with partners in foreign countries who are far away from you, if you don't know him or her very well, then you should do credit inquiry about him or her in case you are cheated by him or her.

How to do Credit Inquiry

1) Through bank and company which have business relations with them.
2) Through offices abroad.
3) Through commercial chamber and professional offices (inquiry agency) on credit inquiry.

Content for Credit Inquiry

It is very important to get the necessary information about the company concerning 4Cs (credit, character, capital, capacity), which means you should know about its reputation, financial status and business mode before conducting a transaction, especially the one that requires a large sum of money.

The Structure of Letters of Credit Inquiry

Taking some correspondences as samples, content of correspondence about credit inquiry is generally made up of the following parts:

Part One

调查的原因，并表明目的，要求得到某一公司的资信资料。

e. g. We are pleased to receive....   我们高兴地收到……

Part Two

进入询问的有关主题，请对方直言相告。

e. g. Will you kindly send us...;   劳驾给我们寄来……好吗？

As soon as these inquires have been satisfactorily settled, ...;
这些查询一经圆满解决，就……

For safety's sake, we should like to know...   安全起见，我们应该知晓……

Part Three

保证保密。

e. g. In confidence, ...   秘密地，……

Part Four

说些感激的话，表示感激和诚意。

e. g. We sincerely hope that ....   我们真诚地希望……

✓ Lead In — Dialogues

The manager of a Chinese mold company, Zhou Lin (A) is asking Bank of China (B) to make a credit investigation into their counterpart.

A: Good afternoon, Miss. I'm here asking for your help.
B: What's it, please?

Situation 2　Establishing Business Relations

A: Our company is about to establish business relations with a new customer, the ABC Engineering Company of New Zealand. I mean my company is to export a number of mold products to the company and the company suggested on effecting payment by time L/C.

B: I see. You want our bank to make an investigation of the financial position of that company?

A: Yes, we want you to make a credit investigation for our company.

B: Please fill out this form with detailed information, such as the full name of the company, the opening bank and the account number.

A: Here you are.

B: Oh, it's the National Bank of New Zealand. Our bank has correspondent relations with it. It can help us.

A: Great! Do you have relations with all the foreign banks in the world? And how much should I pay now?

B: RMB 200 in advance. Our bank has relations with most of the foreign banks in the world, not all.

A: When can I get the result?

B: About one week. I'll call you.

A: Thank you for your help.

B: You're welcome.

Performing

 Text

Sample 1　Credit Inquiry

Dear Sirs,

　　We are going to set up business relations with a new customer, the ABC Engineering Company of New Zealand, which has given us your name as bank reference. Before we decide to sign the contract, we should be obliged if you could let us have your opinion on their reputation and their financial credit standing.

　　Any information you kindly give us will be treated as strictly confidential and without responsibility on your bank.

Yours respectfully,
Zhu Lin
Blue Sky Mold Company

Sample 2 Favorable Reply from the Bank

Dear Sirs,

We are pleased to send you, in confidence, the credit information you requested concerning ABC Engineering Company of New Zealand in your letter of May 12, 2016.

The above firm enjoys the fullest respect and unquestionable confidence in the business world. They are prompt and punctual in all their transactions, and we have no hesitation in giving them credit to an amount considerably beyond the sum you mentioned. However, this is without obligation on our part.

We hope this information may be of use to you.

Yours sincerely,
National Bank of New Zealand

Sample 3 Reply to Credit Inquiry

Dear Sirs,

We are very pleased to receive your order for our goods to the value of（价值为……）USD 25,000. As this is our first transaction with you, will you kindly send us the names of firms or banks to whom reference can be made?（make reference to 提到，涉及）

As soon as these inquires have been satisfactorily settled, we shall be pleased to ship your order. We sincerely hope that this is the beginning of a long and pleasant business relationship. We shall certainly do our best to make it so.

Yours faithfully,

Notes

1) standing *n.* 地位，身份，名誉

   men of high standing 地位高的人

   credit and financial standing 资信状况

2) credit *n.* 信用，赊购，贷款

   financial position and credit standing 资信状况

   e.g. They refused to grant us long-term credits.

   他们拒绝给我们长期贷款。

   No credit is given at this shop.

   这家商店概不赊欠。

   How much do I have to my credit?

   我的存款中还有多少余额？

3) obliged *adj.* 感激的

e. g. We shall be obliged if you could send us your price list as soon as possible.

如果你方能尽快寄来价目表，我方将不胜感激。

4) as reference 作为参考

for your reference 供你方参考

with reference to 就……而言，关于

5) reserve *n.* 储备物，备用金

e. g. We have a reserve of these goods, but it is rather limit.

这些货物我们有些存货，但是很有限。

As I require money quickly I must draw on my reserve.

由于我急于用钱，我必须取出存款。

Practicing

I. Translate the following expressions into English.

资信状况   作为参考

无约束力   储备金

信誉良好   超出你们所提金额

商业信用调查   信用咨询组

以…的信誉   开始调查

II. Translate the following into Chinese.

Report on the Charters Trading Company

This is a report on The Carters Trading Company, LLC about which you inquired in your letter of June 28, 2017. We are pleased to send you the following information.

1. This firm was established by Carter in 1976.

2. It operates as a wholesaler of Canned Foodstuffs which is distributed throughout Canada.

3. The net worth is in excess of USD 8,000,000.

4. The annual business turns over USD 960,000,000.

5. Our records show that they have never failed to meet our bills since they opened an account with us in July 1989. The monthly limit of credit we feel that we may safely grant them is approximately USD 2,000,000.

The managing staff of the company is well known to us and we have high regard for their character, integrity and reliability.

We hope that this information will be of assistance.

Ruder Brian, Manager

The Chatered Bank

III. Write a letter to make a credit investigation of your counterpart from the Commercial Counselor's Office.

Supplement

Supplementary Reading

1. Letter: An Unfavorable Reply

Dear Sirs,

We have received your letter of May 12, 2016, respecting the standing of ABC Engineering Company of New Zealand.

We regret to say that we have to make in reply an unfavorable communication to you. The mentioned firm is known to be heavily committed and have overrun their reserves. They are being pressed by several creditors and their position is precarious. Caution is advisable.

Please consider this information as given in strict confidence.

Yours faithfully,

National Bank of New Zealand

2. Account Inquiry

Definition of "Account Inquiry"

An account inquiry is a review of any type of account, whether it be a depository account or credit account. The inquiry can refer to past records, payments or other specific transactions, or any other entries relating to the account.

Breaking down "Account Inquiry"

Most financial institutions have a formal department that deals with account inquiries. Sometimes the term is used when there is a request to or from a credit agency about a particular consumer.

An account inquiry could be done per the request of a bank, lender, or other financial institution that requires a copy of an account history when an individual, business, or other entity applies for credit or a loan. Credit agencies may issue account inquiries to credit card companies or other lenders as part of assessing whether they are current on the bills they are responsible for.

Why Account Inquiries Are Performed

Account inquiry may typically be initiated when an individual seeks to take on new debt, particularly in conjunction with making a substantial purchase such as the acquisition of real estate. Before the individual is approved for the new debt, the lender wants to see the track record of the applicant when it comes to paying their debts in an orderly fashion. This is a step in assessing the overall creditworthiness of a potential borrower, as well as structuring the rates they may be offered for the loan they are seeking.

An account holder may initiate an account inquiry themselves, particularly if questionable activity is suspected. For instance, if there are debits that the account holder does not recall authorizing, an inquiry can provide answers to where the charges originate from. This could be a step in identifying security breaches or instances of fraud by bringing attention to transactions that are not familiar. The account holder could request that bank or creditor launch an investigation into such transactions.

Account inquiries might also be made to ensure that payments that are owed have cleared and were delivered on time.

Excessive account inquiries by third parties, particularly for credit cards, may have an adverse effect on the credit rating of an individual. If an individual applies for multiple credit cards in a short period of time, each application will usually trigger an account inquiry into their payment history.

When those inquiries are reported to credit agencies, it may be regarded as a form of high risk and a cause to lower the consumer's credit score.

✔ Knowledge Link

☆ 企业资信状况

企业资信状况主要包括企业的资金和信用这两个方面。资金是指企业的注册资本、财产以及资产负债情况等；信用是指企业的经营作风、履约信誉等。这是客户资信调研的主要内容，特别对中间商更应重视。例如，有的客户愿意洽谈上亿美元的投资项目，但经调研其注册资本只有几十万美元。对这样的客户，就该考虑其资信能力。

☆ 企业资信调查

企业资信调查是一种对被调查企业的资产进行的调查。资信调查工作能了解投资对象的投资环境或合作伙伴的真实情况。借此判断其信用的优劣，并作为决定授信或是否合作的依据。

☆ 企业资信调查内容

一、企业基本工商情况调查及核验

企业基本工商情况是指在工商局查询到的目标企业基本情况，主要包括发起股东情况、股东结构及其历史变化、验资机构名称、住所及主要依据、银行基本账户、主管部门、相关政府或上级部门批文、分支机构、对外投资、住所及经营场所、重大登记事项的历次变更、曾任高管人员、企业资产构成及经营概况、章程、营业执照及其他资质文件、企业性质、是否有独立法人资格、历年主要财务报表及特殊情况报告、吊销营业执照及企业注销情况等。多数情况下，企业在工商部门的登记内容由企业工作人员自己填写提交，工商登记部门也不加翔实核查，因此对于这些信息要本着具体问题具体分析的态度，不能轻信，也不能轻易放过任何可能存在的资信线索。目前，企业工商登记电脑查询系统中的企业资料有限，存在查询权限的等级限制，扫描成图像文件时也存在字迹不清、漏页等问题，无法进一步获取更加翔实的信息，因此必要时可考虑查询工商局保存的纸质档案，便于获取更多资信线索。比如，查获企业历年变动的住所或经营场所登记情况后，可询问出租场地方的基层负责人，如负责收取租金的财务部门相关人员。由于基层负责人常年与目标企业打交道，负责收取租金、处理与目标企业的纠纷等，目标企业是否延付、拒付租金，是否经营良好，这些基层负责人员均有详细的第一手资料，极富参考价值。而且，从一些负责追讨租金和提供售后服务的人员处还可查获企业现在的办公场所和法定代表人住址。

有的目标单位连续搬迁办公场所，这属于典型的空壳公司逃债行为，目的在于竭力避免被债权人追及。对这种企业，要考虑同时采取多种渠道探寻，例如通过互联网、查号台、行业协会、企业法定代表人身份证载明住址，以及其他线索延伸搜寻。搜寻时要注意方式方法，保持细心和适当的想象力。如属于建筑行业的企业，就考虑行业特点，通过环保、建设规划等部门搜寻施工现场，进而找到企业当前住址。对企业上级主管部门相关人员、股东或曾任高管人员的延伸调查、谈话询问，只要有适当的方法与手段，也常可获取有用信息。

二、企业真实可变现资产情况的调查及核验

企业资信调查中的核心部分是企业真实可变现资产情况的调查及核验，真实可变现资产的价值及变现速度决定了企业偿债能力的大小。企业真实可变现资产情况包括土地、房产的产权人名称、性质和有无抵押、查封或其他权利限制情况，是否存在产权纠纷或涉诉，机器设备情况，车辆情况以及持有股权、债券或其他金融凭证、票据或其他金融证券资产、其他可变现资产或权利等。

调查过程中要注意登记部门的登记情况可能并不是最终的准确情况，某些相关部门的管理不善，可能导致资料失真。比如，土地、房屋的抵押、查封状况，有可能漏登记，或出现产权单位名称笔误、漏字的情况。在查询时要坚持宽范围原则：查询产权单位名称时尽可能以核心词汇宽范围查询，对同一企业下的所有土地、房产均作权属、抵押两种查询，对企业有其他名称或改制前后、更名前后的不同名称也要一一查询，防止企业实际资产未纳入报告范围，尽量避免遗漏。同时，在出具调查报告时要谨慎用词。

对土地、房产还要进行现场查勘。切实掌握企业土地、房产现状，清晰区分可变现资产范围。如企业拥有产权的土地已经建为家属楼，则将所占土地变现已不具可行性。多做现场查勘询问，还有助于提高土地房产变现的处理效率。对机器设备、车辆的调查要特别注重保持及时控制的可能性。如担保方将机器设备抵押，或法院将机器设备扣押，但作为权益对价方仍无法消除对方擅自处理机器设备的可能。抵押的机器设备无法切实掌握在权利方手中，也就给了抵押方随时将机器设备单方处理的机会。所以，调查时要着重考察机器设备及其附属物的实际可控性。对车辆的调查则要重点审查在车管部门的备案情况及车辆已度过的折旧年限。对调查目标单位持有股权、债券、金融凭证、票据、其他可变现资产或权利的调查工作也要坚持审查其实际可控情况，如不能予以实际有效控制，则应如实写入调查报告，并进一步提出控制建议。

三、企业资信自荐报告的核验

Situation 2 Establishing Business Relations

企业为获得贷款、融资、合作机会或信用评级,常会出具或聘请第三方出具企业资信自荐报告。一般情况下,完整的企业资信自荐报告包括企业基本情况介绍、发展历史、企业上下属体系、管理架构、人力资源状况、商业渠道、主要合作伙伴、过去三年经审计的年度财务报表及最新季报、未来三年发展规划或纲要、所处产业介绍、区域市场情况介绍、企业在行业中的地位、经营业绩、所获荣誉、资金需求及理由、资金投入方向及其梯层进度、收入测算、高管简历、是否有改制情况或历史遗留问题等。

在对企业资信自荐报告的调查中,要重点核验融资目的、资金投向、预期利润与行业或产品平均收益率比较、现金流能力、贷款数额和结构,有无逾期、抵押情况、担保情况、涉诉情况、历年利润分配等,并通过谈话加以核实。

四、其他资信调查工作

在企业资信调查工作中,除以上几方面之外,还可通过一些侧面调查进行配合,以便于全面反映目标单位的完整资信情况。比如,考察企业法人治理结构是否健全、有效,进行上下游企业或上下游产品链调查,进行主要市场竞争对手情况、合同履约情况、有否特殊背景和相关政府主管人员情况调查。此外,还应调查目标企业是否拖欠员工四金及四金缴纳比例,有无职工集资,有无大股东恶意控制或账务混乱情况等。考察时要注意甄别信息,避免受假象干扰。

(资料来源: https://baike.baidu.com/item/%E4%BC%81%E4%B8%9A%E8%B5%84%E4%BF%A1%E8%B0%83%E6%9F%A5/629948?fr=aladdin)

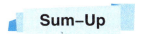

The following sentences are usually used in establishing the business relations.

1. Stating Source of Information

◇ We learn your name and address from…
   我们从……得知贵方的名称和地址。

◇ Through the courtesy of…, we come to know that…
   承蒙……告知,我们得知……

◇ We are indebted for your name to…, who informed us that…
   承蒙……告知你方姓名,他告诉我们……

◇ On the recommendation of…, we have learned that…
   由……推荐,我们得知……

◇ We are given to understand that…
   据了解,……

2. Showing Intension of Establishing the Business Relations

◇ We are writing in the hope of establishing the business relations with you.
   我们写信希望与你方建立贸易关系。

◇ We take this liberty of writing to you with a view of building up the business relations with your firm.

我们冒昧写信以期与贵公司建立业务关系。

◇ The purpose of this letter is to explore the possibilities of developing trade with you.

本信的目的是探索与你们发展贸易的可能性。

3. Making Self-Introduction

◇ Our lines are mainly…

我们经营的业务主要是……

◇ We are a state-owned corporation, handling…

我们是国有企业，经营……

◇ … falls within our business scope.

……属于我方经营范围。

◇ We wish to introduce ourselves as one of the leading importers of…

自我介绍一下，我们是一流的……进口商。

4. Putting Forward Detailed Requirements

◇ We shall be obliged/ grateful if you could…

如果你方能……，我们将非常感激。

◇ We will appreciated it very much if you could…

如果你方能……，我方将不胜感激。

◇ If you are interested in any item, please don't hesitate to contact us.

如果你方对其中任何一种产品感兴趣的话，请立即联系我们。

5. Expressing Expectation

◇ We are looking forward to your early reply.

期盼你方早日回信。

◇ We are anticipating/ awaiting your favorable reply.

静候佳音。

◇ Your early reply will be highly appreciated.

如果你方能早日回信，我方将不胜感激。

Situation 03 Negotiations and Consultations

📝 Objectives

1) To be able to translate and write an enquiry and the reply to it.
2) To be able to translate and write an offer and the counter-offer.

📝 Introduction

In international trade, a good deal will be made after many negotiations. The processes mainly include enquiry, offer, counter-offer, etc.

An enquiry is a request for the trade terms of certain commodity. When the buyer intends to import, he may send out an enquiry to an exporter, inviting a quotation or an offer for the goods he wishes to buy or simply asking for some general information about these goods. An enquiry received from abroad must be answered fully and promptly and cover all the information asked for.

An offer is a promise made to supply goods on terms stated. It is often a reply to an enquiry. Offers can be divided into two types: firm offer and non-firm offer. A firm offer or an offer with engagement is a definite expression that the seller is ready to close business with the buyer on the terms and conditions put forward. It is irrevocable and unchangeable once it is accepted. A non-firm offer is an offer without engagement. The main difference between a firm offer and a non-firm offer is that the former has validity while the latter does not.

A counter-offer is made when the offeree do not agree with the specific terms such as price, packing and shipment mentioned in the prior offer. He will reply with a counter-proposal on those trade terms unacceptable. When a counter-offer is made, the original offer ends.

Generally speaking, the process of offer and counter-offer is a kind of bargaining in

business. Sometimes two parties will repeat the process for several times to complete a transaction. Both parties should pay more attention to the expression they use to avoid misunderstanding.

Main Points of an Enquiry

1) Stating the source of information and intention of writing.

2) Expressing your detailed requirements.

3) Giving reference about the market and price that will be obtained.

4) Showing the wish of early reply or an offer.

Main Points of an Offer

1) Thanking for the enquiry

2) Explaining the details of price, discount, packing, delivery, etc.

3) Showing validity of the offer (if it is a firm-offer)

4) Expressing the hope of acceptance of the offer

Main Points of a Counter-Offer

1) Expressing gratitude to the original offer

2) Explaining the reasons for inability to accept the offer

3) Putting forward a counter-proposal

4) Expecting the acceptance

Task 1 General Enquiry and Reply

Preparing

 What is Enquiry?

An enquiry is a request made by a buyer for goods or services he is interested in.

The aim of making enquiries is to get information about goods to be ordered, inclusive of prices, product specification, packing, discounts, terms of payment, delivery date and other concerns.

Making Enquiries

In international trade, enquiry is the first step of a business negotiation. Enquiry is usually made by the buyer to invite a quotation or offer from the seller in order to buy certain goods or services. Enquiry may be made by mail, e-mail, fax, telephone call, or hand-written note to suppliers through personal contact.

Importance of Making an Enquiry

Enquiry is the basis of transaction, making a very important step of bringing a would-be buyer and a potential seller together in international trade.

It functions as a bridge between a buyer and a seller.

Contents of an Enquiry

In an enquiry, the message conveyed should be simple, clear, reasonable and to be point.

In order to communicate a message, you must try to provide all the necessary information, but it must be clear and as brief as possible.

In addition, adopting an appropriate tone is necessary. A business letter is characterized by a formal and serious tone. Try to be polite, honest and friendly.

An Enquiry is Usually Organized in the Following Steps

1) State how you get to know about the firm.
2) Express your interests in the products produced by the supplier.
3) Provide detailed information to introduce your company.
4) If it is a general enquiry, indicate the general information of the commodity, such as the catalog, samples and the price list; If it is a specific enquiry, appoint a specific commodity and ask for detailed information on specific trade terms, such as specifications, price, terms of payment, delivery date and discount.

Writing Steps

1. Showing Interests in the Products

We are interested in your product.

我方对贵方的产品很感兴趣。

Some of our clients show interest in your products and wish to have your quotations.

我方一些客户对贵方的产品有兴趣,并希望获知贵方报价。

2. Making Enquiries

Please send us samples and quote us your lowest price FOB Tokyo for each of the following items.

请贵方寄来以下每样商品的样品并报最低的东京船上交货价。

We shall appreciate it very much if you will send us a copy of the price list of your products.

请贵方寄来一份产品价格单，我方将不胜感激。

3. Expressing Hopes or Wishes

Please give this enquiry your prompt attention.

请贵方对此询盘尽快回复。

We hope this will be a good start for long and mutually profitable business relations.

我方希望这将是双方长期互利贸易关系的良好开端。

General Enquiry

General Enquiry 一般询盘

States clearly all the information he needs, including general information, a catalogue, a pricelist, a sample and etc.

"First Enquiry"

A first enquiry is also called an outgoing enquiry. It is an enquiry sent to suppliers who has not previously dealt with.

A First Enquiry Should

1) Tell the correspondent or prospective supplier how his name is obtained.

2) Identify yourself.

3) Indicate clearly the information you are after. (The quantities needed, the models desired, the usual terms of trade, etc.)

Some Rules to Follow in Enquiry Letters

1) Address your enquiry letters to the company rather than to an individual.

2) Should be clear and to the point.

—Keep your questions to a minimum.

—Number your questions if you get more than three to ask.

—One paragraph for one point/topic; desirable one letter for one issue.

3) Coherence — Link each sentence to the preceding one; be sure that paragraphs are linked, too.

4) Emphasis — Put what you want to emphasize in an emphatic position.

Sentence Linked

We want to relieve this situation. We are asking to establish a direct business relation with your corporation.

In order to relieve this situation, we are asking to establish a direct business relation with your corporation.

Emphatic Position

Also, by separate post, we are sending you some samples and feel confident that when you have examined them you will agree that the goods are both excellent in quality and reasonable in price.

✓ Lead In — Dialogues

Mr. Anderson (A), president of Tianjin Machine Tools Corporation, is now having a general discussion with a Canadian importer Mr. Black (B). Black wants to make some enquiries about some machines.

A: I believe you have seen our exhibits in the sample room. What do you think of them? What is it, in particular, you are interested in?

B: I have a great interest in your machine tools. Some of our customers have recently expressed interest in your products, so I think some of the items may find a ready market in our county.

A: Okay. Now, we'd like to know if you have any specific requirement in mind.

B: Here is a list of my requirements. I'd like to have your lowest quotation, FOB Tianjin.

A: Thank you for your enquiry. Our price is different according to the size of the order. Would you tell us what quantity you require so that we can work out the offers?

B: I'll do that. But could you give me indication of price? I must make it clear that if your price is competitive, we'll place large orders with you.

A: Thank you. I'll prepare for it and give it to you tomorrow.

B: That's okay. See you tomorrow.

Performing

Text

Sample 1　General Enquiry

Dear Sirs,

　　We have seen your advertisement in the Trade Directory No. 2.

　　We are very interested in your pure cotton shirts and should be obliged if you would send us by return your illustrated catalogue and price list of the goods.

　　We are looking forward to receiving your prompt reply.

Yours sincerely,

Sample 2　Reply to the Above

Dear Sirs,

　　We thank you for your inquiry of March 11.

　　In accordance with your request, we are sending you a copy of our illustrated catalogue together with a range of samples of pure cotton shirts.

　　The price of this article must be revised soon on account of the recent rise in the cost of raw materials.

　　We sincerely hope to be of service to you soon.

Yours faithfully,

Sample 3　General Enquiry

Dear Sirs,

　　Mrs. Brown of this city inform us that you are exporters of all cotton bed-sheets and pillowcases. We would like you to send us details of your various ranges, including sizes, colors and prices, and also samples of the different qualities of material used.

　　We are large dealers in textiles and believe there is a promising market in our area for moderately priced goods of the kind mentioned.

　　When replying, please state your terms of payment and discount you would allow on purchase of quantities of not less than 100 dozen of individual items. Prices quoted should include insurance and freight to Liverpool.

Yours faithfully,

Situation 3 Negotiations and Consultations

Notes

1) be obliged 感激（常用于请求对方做某事）
   类似的表达还有：
   We should be thankful if you would... 如果你方愿意……，我们应该心存感激。
   We should appreciate it if you would... 如果你方愿意……，我方应该不胜感激。
   We should be grateful if you would... 如果你方愿意……，我方应该不胜感激。

2) by return 立即，收信后立即
   e. g. We will quote our favorable price by return.
   我们将会立即报出最优惠价。

3) illustrated adj. 有插图的，有说明的
   e. g. There are the latest types of products mentioned in the enclosed illustrated catalogue.
   随附的插图商品目录里，有我公司的最新几类产品。
   illustration n. 插图，说明，说明书
   illustrate v. 说明

4) in accordance with 符合，与……相一致
   类似的表达还有 "in compliance with"

5) a range of 一套，一系列

6) revise 修改，修正
   revised adj. 经过修改的，修正的
   e. g. Airmail revised price list but full range sample within fortnight.
   航空寄上订正价格表，全套样品两周内寄出。

7) on account of 为了……的缘故
   on account of limited supply 由于供应有限
   e. g. On account of a mistaken calculation, the price is wrong.
   由于计算有误，价格是错的。

8) raw material 原材料

9) be of service to 有助于，对……有用
   e. g. Hope that our service is of service to you.
   希望我们的建议对你们有用。

Practicing

I. Translate the following expressions into English.

一般询盘   插图目录

原材料　　　　　　　　　　从……获悉

立即回复　　　　　　　　　稳定的需求

质量上乘　　　　　　　　　常规订单

具体询盘　　　　　　　　　与……相一致

II. Choose the best answer to complete each of the following sentences.

1. The letter we sent last week is an enquiry _____ color TV sets.

   A. about　　　　B. for　　　　　C. of　　　　　　D. as

2. We produce decorative fabrics _____ different kinds.

   A. in　　　　　B. of　　　　　C. for　　　　　　D. with

3. We thank you for your letter of May 18 and the _____ catalogue.

   A. sent　　　　B. enclosed　　　C. given　　　　　D. presented

4. Your full cooperation _____.

   A. will be thanked very much　　　B. is to be appreciated

   C. is to appreciate　　　　　　　　D. will be highly appreciated

5. While _____ an enquiry, you ought to enquire into quality, specification and price, etc.

   A. making　　　B. offering　　　C. sending　　　　D. giving

6. _____ your Enquiry No. 123, we are sending you a catalog and a sample book for your reference.

   A. According　　B. As per　　　C. As　　　　　　D. About

7. Thank you for your letter of December 11, _____ for peanuts.

   A. inviting　　　B. expecting　　C. enquiring　　　D. asking

8. There is a _____ for Chinese cotton in our market.

   A. great need　　B. increasing need　C. steady demand　D. risen demand

9. Please send us your _____ catalogue.

   A. illustrate　　B. illustrated　　C. illustrating　　D. illustration

10. We will place an order _____ fairly large numbers.

    A. of　　　　　B. with　　　　C. for　　　　　　D. under

III. Translate the following sentences into Chinese.

1. Please send us a sample of each of the items listed above.

2. Would you please let us know if these goods are still available?

3. Please quote us your lowest price with the best discount and the date of delivery.

4. We are enclosing herewith an enquiry sheet.

5. As soon as we have received your enquiry, we will immediately mail you the samples and offer you the most favorable prices.

Situation 3　Negotiations and Consultations

IV. Translate the following letter into English.

敬启者：

很高兴收到你方 8 月 19 日的询价，根据你方要求，现寄上带插图的目录册及价格表。另邮寄上一些样品，相信经查阅后，你方会同意我方产品质量上乘，价格合理。

如果每个款式的购买数量不少于 1,000 件的话，我们可给 2% 的折扣。

早复为盼。

谨上

V. Write a letter about general inquiry（open）.

Supplement

✓ Supplementary Reading

1. Letter

Dear Sirs,

　　We are glad to inform you that we are very much interested in your bicycles for both men and women, and also for children. There is a steady demand here for bicycles of high quality. We are the leading bicycle dealers in this city, where cycling is popular, and have branches in three neighbor districts.

　　Will you please send us a copy of your catalogue for bicycles, with details of your prices and terms of payment? If the quality of your bicycles is high and the prices are reasonable, we will place regular orders for fairly large numbers.

Yours faithfully,

2. Sentences About Credit Enquiry

1) Through the courtesy of ... we learn that you are one of the leading importers of ...in your country and wish to enter into business relations with us.

　　由于……的好意，我方获悉贵方是贵国……最大的进口商之一，欲与贵方建立贸易关系。

2) We owe your name and address to the Chamber of Commerce in your country, through who we learned that you are in the market for silk product.

　　承蒙贵国商会的介绍，我们得知贵公司想要购买丝绸制品。

3) We got the information from our sales manager that you have the desire to cooperate with our firm in marketing our silk products.

　　从我方销售经理处得知，贵方愿与我公司合作销售我们的丝织产品。

4) We are willing to enter into business relations with you on the basis of equality, mutual benefit and exchanging needed goods.

我方愿与贵方在平等互利、互通有无的基础上建立业务关系。

5) We are glad to send you this letter, hoping that it will be the prelude to our friendly business cooperation in the coming years.

我们欣然寄发这封信,希望这会成为未来几年里我们友好商务合作的前奏。

6) We are one of the largest …importers in our country and have handled various kinds of the products for about…years.

我方是我们国内……最大的进口商之一,已经营各类产品达……年。

7) Our corporation is a group enterprise integrating scientific research, business, production and service. As a joint venture, our corporation has won a prominent position in the field of agricultural products in China.

我公司是一家集科学研究、商贸、生产和服务于一体的企业集团。作为一家合资企业,公司已经在中国农产品领域赢得显著地位。

8) We invite you to send us details and prices, possibly also samples, of such goods as you would be interested in selling, and we shall gladly study the sales possibilities in our market.

我们邀请贵方将你方感兴趣销售的商品的详细资料和价格发送给我们,如果可以,将样品也发送给我们,我们很乐于研究其在我方市场上销售的可能性。

9) We look forward to receiving your order and meanwhile enclose a copy of our catalogue as we feel you may be interested in some of our other products.

我们盼望收到贵方订单,同时随函附上一份目录,因为我们认为贵方会对我们的其他产品感兴趣。

10) In recent years the company has experienced a serious difficulty in finance and delayed in executing their normal payment. We would suggest you to pay more attention to the business with them. However, this is just our personal opinion and we wish you to make further investigation.

最近几年该公司在财务上经历严重危机而延误正常的付款,谨建议贵公司与其谨慎交易,此乃我们个人意见,希望贵公司作进一步调查。

11) We take the liberty of writing to you with a view to building up business relations with your firm.

我们冒昧通信,以期与你公司建立业务关系。

12) We have the pleasure of introducing ourselves to you with the hope that we may have an opportunity of cooperating with you in your business extension.

我们有幸自荐,盼望能有机会与你们合作,扩大业务。

13) We are looking forward to your early reply.
    期盼贵方早日回复。
14) Your early reply will be highly appreciated.
    如能早日回复，我方将不胜感激。
15) Awaiting your favorable reply.
    期盼佳音。
16) The above information is given confidentially and without responsibility on our part.
    对以上情况请保守秘密，我方对此不负责任。
17) We are glad to send you this introductory letter, hoping that it will be the prelude to mutually beneficial relations between us.
    我们欣然寄发这些自荐信，希望是互利关系的前奏。
18) The purpose of this letter is to explore the possibilities of developing trade with you.
    本信目的是探索与你们发展贸易的可能性。

✔ Knowledge Link

☆ 同业名录（Trade Directory）

名录是指汇集机构名、人名、地名等基本情况和资料的工具书，具有简明、新颖、确实等特点。名录是一种事实便览性的工具书，虽只提供有关机构、人物等的简要资料，但能起指引情报源的作用，对沟通信息、促进交流、加强协作提供了很大的方便。

同业名录，又称行业名录，是商业、企业性的名录，通常按字顺或分类排列，提供某行业中相关企业的地址、负责人、简况及其他有关信息。

同业名录来源于各种信息渠道，如统计部门、管理部门、行业协会、金融机构及相关报刊等。

Task 2 Specific Enquiry and Reply

📝 Preparing

Specific Enquiry

Points out what products he wants, and may ask for a catalogue, a pricelist, samples, etc, or ask for an offer.

Specific Enquiry Include the Following

1. The names and descriptions of the goods enquired for, including specifications, quantity, etc.

2. Asking whether there is a possibility of giving a special discount and what terms of payment and time of delivery you would expect.

3. Stating the possibility of placing an order.

The differences Among General Enquiry, Specific Enquiry and First Enquiry

General enquiry—general information about goods, catalogs, pricelist, sample, illustrated photo prints, no intention to do business right away.

Specific enquiry—to the exporter or supplier whom you have already set up the business relations. Request for detailed information about the goods: name, specification, price, delivery date, etc.

First enquiry—to a supplier not previously dealt with, intention to establish business relations must be contained. Consequently, telling him how you obtained his name and the introduction to your business such as business scope. The kind of goods handled, quantities and usual terms will be included in your message. This will enable the supplier to decide what he can do for you.

✓ Lead In — Dialogues

Mr. David Kinch (A) and Mr. Yu Ming (B) begin to get down to the brass tracks.

A: I see you're in the line of electronic products.

B: Yes, and I've come to enquire about your computers.

A: I'll be glad to help you. What interests you?

B: Frankly, I really don't know much about your COMPAQ 1200 computers. Could you tell me something about them?

A: With pleasure. These are our latest products and the best selling goods. Here are our samples and catalogs. You'll find all the details from them.

B: Thank you very much.

A: Would you please tell me your specific requirements?

B: I wonder whether you can quote us on FOB basis.

A: Yes. We can give you prices both FOB and CIF. You can compare them and see for yourself which price is better for you.

B: Good. Now, I have another point. Do you allow me a discount?

A: Yes. Our regular practice is 2% trade discount.
B: Before I place an order, I'd like a firm offer in order for us to find time to market the product.
A: Our offers are usually good for 5 days.
B: Thank you very much, Mr. Kinch. What about payment?
A: Our terms of payment are by irrevocable L/C payable by sight draft against presentation of shipping documents.
B: Could you accept Documents against Acceptance?
A: We only accept payment by confirmed irrevocable letter of credit payable by draft at sight.
B: Would it be possible for me to have a closer look at your samples?
A: You are welcome. I'll take you to our showroom.

Performing

Text

Sample 1　Specific Enquiry for Portable Computers

Dear Sirs,

We are pleased to learn from your letter of July 18 that, as manufacturer of computers, you are desirous of entering into direct business relations with us. This is just our desire, too.

We have studied your catalogue and are interested in your portable computer Model PH-88. Please quote us your lowest price, CIF Guangzhou, inclusive of our 2% commission, stating the earliest date of shipment.

Should your price be found competitive and delivery date acceptable, we intend to place a large order of 500 sets with you.

Please give us your reply as soon as possible.

Yours sincerely,

Sample 2　Reply to the Above

Dear Sirs,

Thank you for your letter dated July 18 in which you expressed your interest in our portable computer Model PH-88.

The enclosed brochure will give you detailed information about the Model PH-88 computer. Under cover, we are sending you our offer on CIF Guangzhou, for shipment in September. Usually, we require an irrevocable L/C by draft at sight.

Portable computer Model PH-88 is our latest product. Because of its excellent quality and low price, you can rest assured that it will help you expand your market.

We are looking forward to your trial order.

                                                         Yours sincerely,

Sample 3　Special Enquiry

Dear Sirs,

We have seen your advertisement in "The Economic Daily" in March this year and are interested in your leather boxes and shoes of all kinds.

Please quote us for the supply of the item listed on the enclosed query form, giving your prices CIF Shanghai. Please send us full details of your goods, your earliest delivery and discounts for regular purchases.

As our annual requirements in leather sundries of all kinds are considerable, perhaps you would also send us your catalog and details of your specifications.

We look forward to your early reply.

                                                         Yours faithfully,

Notes

1) be desirous of sth.　　想要某物

    be desirous of doing sth.　　渴望做某事

    be desirous to do sth.　　渴望做某事

    desire　*n.* 渴望，愿望

2) portable computer　　手提电脑

3) quote　*v.* give price for 报价

    e. g.　We hope that you could quote us the lowest price for cotton.

        我们希望你方给我们报棉布的最低价。

        Please quote us 100 metric tons CFR price.

        请报100公吨成本加运费价。

4) inclusive of　　将……考虑在内，包含

5) under cover　　随函

    under separate cover　　另封

6) irrevocable L/C by draft at sight　　不可撤销的即期信用证

7) CIF（Cost, Insurance and Freight）　成本，保险费加运费（俗称"到岸价"）

8) commission　*n.* 佣金

Situation 3　Negotiations and Consultations

commission　作佣金讲时，一些习惯用法如下：

a. 百分之几佣金：a commission of ...% 或 ...% commission

b. 你方/我方百分之几佣金：your/our commission of ...% 或 your/our ...% commission

c. 两笔或几笔佣金：two or several items of commission

d. 一切佣金或各项佣金：all commissions

e. 在每笔生意中抽取5%的佣金：draw (receive) a commission of 5% on each sale

　　e. g. The above price includes your 2% commission.

　　　　以上所开价格包括你方2%的佣金。

Practicing

I. Translate the following expressions into Chinese.

competitive price　　　　　　　enquiry sheet

sample books　　　　　　　　enclosed please find

terms and conditions　　　　　prompt attention

inclusive of　　　　　　　　　under cover

II. Fill in the blanks with proper forms of given words.

quote　enclose　expand　detail　ship

1. It would be very much appreciated if you could confirm the _____ as soon as possible.

2. We wish to get from you more information about the item, please send us the _____ illustration.

3. We trust you will find our _____ satisfactory and look forward to receiving your initial order.

4. We are _____ two copies of our sales contract.

5. We are looking forward to _____ the business with you.

III. Complete the following letter by translating Chinese into English.

Dear sir,

　　Our market is in need of handicraft articles in Canada. As _____ _____ (有稳定的需求) here for high quality Chinese handicrafts, we would like you to send us as soon as possible your catalogues, _____ (样品以及有关产品的所有必要信息). Meanwhile please quote us your _____ _____ (温哥华CIF最低价，并说明最早的船期)。

Should your quality be suitable and the price competitive, _____
_____ (我们将至少向贵公司订购 5,000 件).

_____ (及时关注此事) will be much appreciated.

Yours faithfully,

IV. Writing practice.

1. Write a Letter Stating the Following Points

   1) The name of commodity you want to purchase: suitcases.
   2) You ask for the following information:
      a. price list.
      b. payment terms.
      c. delivery date.
      d. other information.

2. Write a letter about Reply to Specific Enquiry

Re: "Australian Royal" Wool Blanket

We are now considering buying large quantities of your "Australian Royal" wool blanket. There is always a ready market here for "Australian Royal" wool blanket, provided it is of good quality and competitive price. We should be thankful if you would send us its full details concerning the price, discount, term of payment, delivery date, packing and so on. It would also be appreciated if you could forward your samples.

When quoting, please let us have your prices on both FOBC 3% Keelung and CIFC 3% Hong Kong. If your terms are favorable, we shall probably order about 10,000 dozens and open L/C in your favor in time.

We look forward to hearing from you by return.

Yours faithfully,
M&N Company
(signature)
Manager

Supplement

1. Letter 1: Tabulated Enquiry

Dear Sirs,

Re: Stainless Steel Table Ware

We are desirous of having your lowest quotation for the above article on the terms and conditions mentioned below, to which your prompt attention is requested:

Name of the commodity: Stainless steel table ware

Quantity required: 1,000 sets

Price: CFR Kobe including cost of suitable packing for export

Terms of Payment: By confirmed and irrevocable L/C

Time of Shipment: June / July 2001

We trust that you will send us your reply soon.

Yours faithfully,

2. Letter 2: Special Enquiry

Dear sirs,

We are glad to learn from your letter of March 20, as exporters of Chinese Silk Piece Goods, you intend to establish direct business connections with us which happens to be our desire.

At present, we are interested in Crepe Georgette and please let us have your lowest CIFC 3% Lagos together with your terms of payment and state whether you would be able to effect delivery one month after receiving our order.

In order to acquaint us with the material and workmanship of your products, we shall be pleased if you could send us your catalogues, sample books and all necessary information on Crepe Georgette.

Should your price be found competitive and delivery date is acceptable, we intend to place a substantial order.

Your early reply will be highly appreciated.

Yours truly,

3. Example Sentences

1) We read with interest your advertisement in *China Daily* and should be glad to receive particulars of your tender for port construction.

   我们对你方在《中国日报》上刊登的广告很感兴趣，现请你方寄送港口建设投标的详细情况。

2) We are interested in the mechanical toys demonstrated at the recent Guangzhou Trade Fair and should be glad to have details of your export terms.

   我们对你最近在广州交易会上展列的机械玩具感兴趣，请详告你方出口条件。

3) We have seen your advertisement in the "Foreign Trade" and should be glad if you would send us by return patterns and prices of good quality cottons available from stock.

   我们已经看到了贵方在"对外贸易"上的广告，如果你方能够给我们发送优等棉花的现货来样和价格，我们将很高兴。

4）We were pleased to know from your letter of 24th June of your interest in our products and enclose the catalogue and price list giving the details you asked for. Also enclosed you will find details of our conditions of sale and terms of payment.

我们很高兴地从你方6月24日的来信中获悉，你方对我们的产品感兴趣，附函的目录和价格单给出了你方要求的详细资料，同时附有我方的销售条件和支付条件。

5）We are making you the following offer, subject to your reply reaching here within five days.

我们作如下报价，以你方5天内回复为准。

6）We shall be pleased if you will furnish us with your lowest quotation for the following goods.

如果你们为我们提供下列产品的最低报价，我们将会很高兴。

7）If you think this offer is acceptable to you, please fax us immediately for our confirmation.

如果你方认为此报价对你方是可以接受的，请立即向我们发出传真以便我们确认。

8）Under separate cover, we are sending you one sample pad for the synthetic fabric dress materials we are exporting at present. We hope some of the designs and colors will prove to your liking.

另行寄上我方目前出口的合成纤维衣料，希望某些花样及颜色能使你喜欢。

9）We have been importers of …… for many years. At present, we are interested in extending our range and would appreciate your catalogues and quotations.

多年来，我公司经营……进口生意。现欲扩展业务范围，盼能惠寄商品目录和报价单。

10）We specialize in supplying small stores in rural areas. Over 3,000 of these stores virtually depend on us, and this assured sales outlet enables us to dispose of fairly large quantities.

我们专向乡镇小商店供货。3,000家以上此种商店靠我们供货，这些有保证的销路足使我们能大量推销。

11）Your samples should give us an idea of the colors and quality of the products.

你公司寄来的样品，使我们对你公司产品的色彩与品质有一番了解。

12）We cannot take anything off the price.

此价不能再减。

13）One of our clients has sent us a quotation for 2,000 units of refrigerator to be sold in the countries in south-east Asia. Please quote us your best terms CIF Manila and let us know what quantities you are able to deliver at regular intervals.

我方一客户发来询盘，要求2,000台销往东南亚国家的电冰箱报价，请报贵方CIF马尼拉最优惠交易条件，并请告知贵方能定期提供的数量。

14) We have the pleasure of sending you a direction of how to operate our new dishwashing machine.
现寄上关于如何使用我们新式洗碗机的说明书一份。
15) If the prices quoted are competitive/workable, and the quality up to standard, we will place orders on a regular basis.
如果贵方报价有竞争力/可行性,产品质量达标,我方将长期订购。
16) We trust you will give this enquiry your immediate attention and let us have your reply at an early date.
我方相信贵方会对此询盘予以重视并及早回复。
17) We have been informed by the Bank of Canada, Vancouver that you are one of the leading exporters of textiles in Shanghai.
加拿大银行温哥华分行告知我们,你公司是上海的主要纺织品出口商之一。
18) We are on the look-out for the following items and should be grateful if you would send samples of the same.
我们欲求购下列产品,如贵公司能寄来样品,我们将非常感激。
19) In reply to your enquiry dated November 25, we are sending you here with our quotation, along with various samples of leather gloves closely resembling to what you want.
应贵公司 11 月 25 日来函询问,现寄上我方的报价和几副式样不同的与贵方要求近似的皮手套样品。
20) You will find that we have given you the most favored quotation for the same products.
你将会发现,我们给贵公司的报价是相同产品中最低的。

✔ Knowledge Link

☆ 外贸询盘回复技巧

供应商给买方回复邮件时,要尽量遵循以下五大要诀。

全面:要全面彻底地回答买家查询的方方面面,包括买家所有的问题和感兴趣的点点滴滴。

准确:要将回复信写得很清楚,首先要正确理解买家来函的准确意思;其次,供应商要多使用有说服力、准确的数据,切忌使用模棱两可或含糊的词语和内容。

清楚:邮件不论是排版还是语句都应整洁明了,避免使用难懂的词语或表达方法。

具体:给买家回复的信息无疑越具体越好,这样能方便买家做出决策。

礼貌:要多使用正式的表达,少用口语语气,尊重对方的风土人情、禁忌和宗教信仰。

☆ 询价文件涉及的主要内容

一、询价项目的"品名"或"料号"

二、询价项目的"数量"

三、询价项目的"规格书"

四、询价项目的"品质"要求

Task 3　Firm Offer

Preparing

Relative Reading

What is Offer?

An offer is a promise to supply goods on the terms stated. It is always made by the seller and reply to the enquiry.

The person making the offer is called "offeror（报盘人）", while the person receiving the offer is called "offeree（受盘人）".

A Satisfactory Quotation will Include the Followings

a. An expression of thanks for the enquiry

b. Details of prices, discounts and terms of payment

c. A statement of what the prices cover (e. g. freight and insurance, etc.)

d. An undertaking as to date of delivery or time of shipment

e. The period for which the quotation is valid

What is a Firm Offer?

A firm offer is a promise to sell goods at a stated price, usually within a stated period of time. It must be clear, definite, complete and final.

A firm offer is an offer that will remain open for a certain period or until a certain time or happening of a certain event, during which it is incapable of being revoked. As a general rule, all offers are revocable at any time prior to acceptance, even those offers that purport to be irrevocable on their face.

In the United States, an exception is the merchant firm offer rule set out in Uniform Commercial Code — § 2-205, which states that an offer is firm and irrevocable if it is an offer to buy or sell goods made by a merchant and it is in writing and signed by the offeror. Such an offer is irrevocable even in the absence of consideration. If no time is stated, it is irrevocable for a reasonable time, but in no event may a period of irrevocability exceed three months. Any such term of assurance in a form supplied by the offeree must be separately signed by the offeror. However, even when the period of irrevocability expires, the offer may still remain open until revoked or rejected according to the general rules regarding termination of an offer.

If the offeree rejects, fails to accept the terms of the offer, fixed or otherwise, or makes a counter-offer, then the original offer is terminated.

The Difference between an Offer and a Quotation

A quotation is not an "offer" in the legal sense. It is just an indication of price without contractual obligation and subject to change without previous notice.

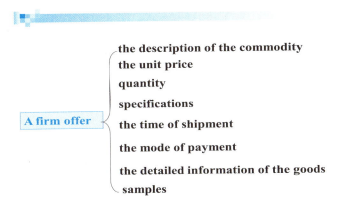

A firm offer
- the description of the commodity
- the unit price
- quantity
- specifications
- the time of shipment
- the mode of payment
- the detailed information of the goods
- samples

A firm offer cannot be withdrawn by the seller within its validity. It is the buyer's option to accept, reject or counter-offer during the validity period. If the buyer accepts, then it is a contractual obligation.

So no reputable seller would risk his reputation by withdrawing his offer before the stated time.

When a buyer rejects a quotation, he should write and thank the seller for his trouble and explain the reason for rejection.

✔ Lead In — Dialogues

Mr. David Kinch (A) is now making a firm offer to Mr. Yu Ming (B).

A: I believe you have seen our computer samples in our showroom. May I know what particular items you're interested in?

B: I've seen your samples and studied your catalogs. I think some of the items will find a ready market in China.

A: When can I have your order?

B: Let's settle the prices before placing an order. I hope you will give me your best offer.

A: Would you tell us the quantity you require so as to enable us to work out the offer?

B: If we order 1,000 sets of COMPAQ 1200 computer, what's the best price you'll give then?

A: What's the basis are we to offer, FOB or CIF?

B: I'd like to have your lowest quotation CIF Shanghai.

A: Wait a minute. We'll have it worked out very soon. Have a cup of coffee, please. (after counting) Oh, now I have the offer ready for you. The price for COMPAQ 1200 computer is USD 900 per set CIF Shanghai. The size of order is 1,000 sets. The date of delivery is July.

B: How long does your current offer remain valid?

A: Our offer is firm offer, and remains open for three days. Here is the quotation sheet.

B: OK. We'll give you a reply tomorrow morning.

Performing

Text

Sample 1   Firm Offer

Dear Sirs,

We confirm your letter July 23, 2010, asking us to make you a firm offer for Groundnut CFR Singapore.

We are offering you 3,000 metric tons of Groundnuts, the first grade, at CNY 1,800 net per metric ton CFR Singapore for shipment during October, 2010. This offer is firm, subject to the receipt of your reply before August 10, 2010.

Please note that we have quoted our most favorable price and are unable to entertain any counter-offer.

As you know, there is a heavy demand for groundnut at present and this has resulted in increased prices. It will be to your advantage to place an order without delay.

Looking forward to your reply.

Yours respectfully,

Sample 2   Tabulated Firm Offer

Dear Sirs,

DELL PC

We confirm your fax of August 10, asking us to make you an offer for captioned personal computers, FOB Xingang. Now we are making you an offer as follows:

Commodity: DELL Personal Computer

Specification: CPU Intel Core i3

Quantity: 2,000 sets

Packing: Each set is wrapped in a polybag and packed in a standard export cardboard carton lined with foam.

Shipment: October, 2010

Payment: by confirmed, irrevocable L/C payable by draft at sight which should reach us 30 days before the date of shipment.

This offer is subject to your reply here on or before August 25.

We highly appreciate your early reply.

Yours sincerely,
National Bank of New Zealand

Sample 3   Reply to Firm Offer

Dear Mr. Chen Jian,

We acknowledge receipt of your letter of April 15th, and confirm having faxed you today in reply, as per confirmation copy enclosed. You will note from our fax that we are in a position to offer you 50 tons of copper at the attractive price of Stg. 600 per ton CFR Shanghai for delivery within one month after your placing an order with us. Payment is to be effected by irrevocable L/C at sight in Pounds Sterling in London.

This offer is firm, subject to your immediate reply, which should reach us not later than the end of this month. There is little likelihood of the goods remaining unsold once this particular offer has lapsed.

Yours faithfully,
David Stone

Notes

1) offer   *v.* 报盘，供应，提供   *n.* 报盘

   e.g. We can offer you large quantities of TV sets at attractive prices.
   我们能以很具吸引力的价格给你方报盘大量的电视机。

2) for shipment during...   装运期为……

3) subject to   以……为准，以……为条件

   e.g. The consignments are subject to weather change.
   这批货物很易受天气影响。

   This offer is subject to our final confirmation.

这项发盘以我方最后确认为准。

4) entertain counter-offer 考虑接受还盘

　　entertain *v.* 考虑，接受

　　e. g. we are too heavily committed to be able to entertain fresh orders.

　　　　我们要处理的订单太多，很难再接受新的订货。

5) a heavy demand for 对……有大量需求

6) without delay as soon as possible 毫不耽搁地

7) wrap *vt.* 裹，包，捆

　　wrap a book in a newspaper 把书包在报纸里

8) polybag *n.* 塑料袋

9) standard export cardboard carton 标准出口纸箱

10) line with... 以……填塞

　　e. g. The inside of the box was lined with silk.

　　　　那盒子用丝作衬里。

11) foam *n.* 泡沫，泡沫塑料

Practicing

I. Translate the following expressions into English.

实盘	根据要求
接盘人	立即
最低价	虚盘
按照	以……为准
很大的需求	导致

II. Choose the best answer to complete each of the following sentences.

1. As requested _____ your E-mail of March 1, we are sending you _____ the required quotation sheet.

　　A. in, herewith　　B. for, herewith　　C. for, in　　D. on, herewith

2. Please quote us your lowest prices _____ CIF Singapore basis for men's shirts _____ prompt shipment.

　　A. in, for　　B. from, for　　C. on, for　　D. from, on

3. This offer is subject _____ before July 23.

　　A. for your reply reaches us　　　　B. for your reply reaching us
　　C. to our receiving your reply　　　D. to your reply arriving at us

4. As wholesalers we are _____ to handle large quantities.

A. of a position　　B. in the position　　C. at a position　　D. in a position

5. Shipment is to be made _____ 3 months on receipt of the relative L/C.

　　A. in　　　　　　B. by　　　　　　　C. during　　　　　　D. within

6. We hope you will quote us competitive price _____ Liverpool _____ Printed Shirting.

　　A. of CIF, for　　B. CIF, for　　　　C. of CIF, on　　　　D. CIF, on

7. Could you make us a firm offer _____ shoes?

　　A. of　　　　　　B. for　　　　　　　C. offer　　　　　　D. at

8. We are pleased to inform you that the item you requested can be supplied _____.

　　A. from stock　　B. in stock　　　　C. out of stock　　　D. of stock

9. We acknowledge with thanks _____ your fax of March 2.

　　A. receipt　　　　B. receive　　　　　C. receipt of　　　　D. receiving

10. We confirm _____ purchased 2,000 MP3 Players from you.

　　A. have　　　　　B. having　　　　　　C. to have　　　　　D. have been

III. Fill in the missing words.

Dear sirs,

　　_____ to your enquiry of May 16, we very much _____ that we are unable to make you an offer for above-mentioned goods, mainly _____ to low stock of this _____ in our market. In fact, our _____ are compelled to decline orders because of the _____ of materials.

　　We shall, of course, revert to this matter and cable you offers as _____ as the supply position improves.

　　In the _____, if you should require any other metallic foils, please _____ free to send us your specific enquiries which will _____ our prompt attention.

　　　　　　　　　　　　　　　　　　　　　　　　　　　　　　Yours faithfully,

IV. Writing practice.

1. Write a letter stating the following points.

　　对 3 月 19 日的询盘做出如下报盘：

　　1）商品名称：大豆，2010 年精选货；

　　2）数量：200 公吨；

　　3）价格：成本加运费至纽约，每公吨 1,900 美元；

　　4）装运期：2010 年 8 月；

　　5）支付：2010 年 7 月 15 日前开立并送达我方不可撤销的、以我方为受益人的即期信用证，有效期至装运日后15天在中国广州议付。

2. Write a letter about reply to the enquiry of "Australian Royal" wool blanket stating the following points.

1）感谢之前的询盘；

2）商品的名称、质量、有关价格和折扣等方面；

3）表示希望接受所给报价。

Supplement

Supplementary Reading

1. Letter

Dear sirs,

In reply to your enquiry letter of December 3, we have pleasure in making an offer for teapots.

Besides those advertised in *The Economist*, our illustrated catalog enclosed shows various types of teapots. Most types can be supplied from stock. 45-60 days should be allowed for delivery of those marked with an asterisk.

We can allow a 2% discount on all orders of USD 6,000 in value and over, and a 3% on orders exceeding USD 20,000.

The offer holds good until 4 o'clock p.m. 18th of December, Beijing time.

Looking forward to receiving your order and any orders you place with us will be processed promptly.

Yours faithfully,

2. Reading: A Firm Offer

A firm offer is an irrevocable offer presented in a verified medium which is good for a specific period of time. The offer may be an offer to buy or sell. If accepted, the firm offer is used to develop a contract which can be signed by all parties involved, thus committing them to the agreement. The laws surrounding firm offers vary from nation to nation, but generally the term "firm offer" is used to describe an offer made by a merchant, with the offer being directed at a consumer or another merchant.

Historically, only written and signed offers were considered firm offers. However, the law has shifted in many areas of the world, and today such an offer must simply be "authenticated", allowing for the use of other media. For example, a firm offer may be transmitted electronically with a mark which acts as a signature. The language of the offer must also clearly indicate that it is firm.

Unless specified otherwise, a firm offer lasts 30 days. After this period, the offer is considered void. If a party wants to accept the offer after this period, it must request another offer. The set time period is designed to ensure that the offer is not allowed to float eternally, and to create reasonable expectations and limits for both parties. If a caterer submits a firm offer for a job, for example, it wants to know if it will be rejected so that it can submit other offers for the same period of time and avoid missing out on business while waiting to hear back on an offer.

Both goods and services can be included in a firm offer. The offer usually describes in detail what is being offered and at what price, and provides other specifics which will be used to structure a contract. For example, it might state that a caterer is offering to handle a wedding banquet for 100 people, or that a merchant is offering to purchase a set number of units at a given price.

In the United States, the Uniform Commercial Code (UCC) provides guidelines for firm offers, among many other things. The Code is designed to make sure that commercial transactions are handled consistently and smoothly across the United States, and to confirm that people understand the underlying terms and conditions for contracts, offers, and other activities undertaken by merchants of all sizes.

✔ Knowledge Link

☆ 英国《经济学人》杂志

1843年创刊于英国，是一份包含新闻、政治经济观点和深度分析的周刊。客观公正是《经济学人》杂志的生命所在。公司的构成禁止任何组织或个人获得杂志半数以上的持股权。该杂志所有的文章都不署名，皆由集体创作。

《经济学人》在20世纪20年代发行量仅有3,700份，直到1970年还未能突破10万大关。2007年，杂志分别在7个国家印刷，其发行量已超过70万，其中有4/5的发行量是在英国本土以外，单独在美国的发行量占总量的1/3。

一直以来，《经济学人》秉承了朴实无华的作风，始终恪守创始人James Wilson的办刊思想："在文章中提出的任何争论和主张必须要经得起事实的考验"。

《经济学人》读者定位为高收入、富有独立见解和批判精神的社会精英，与此相适应，文章始终保持了一种独特的格调：不拘一格、叙述朴实、用词准确和忠于事实。

Task 4 Non-Firm Offer

Preparing

✔ Relative Reading

What is Non-Firm Offer?

Contrary to a firm offer, a non-firm offer is an offer without engagement (诺言、承诺). It is unclear, incomplete and with reservation. It has no binding force upon the offeror. The trade terms are not indicated clearly and definitely. The content is not so completed as that of a firm offer. It has no term of validity. Moreover, the offeror makes the offer with reservation: the offer is subject to (受制于……) his final confirmation. So a non-firm offer often bears (带有、具有) such wording (措辞) "this offer is subject to our final confirmation", or "the prices are subject to change without notice".

Firm offer can encourage offerees to make decision and thus close business (达成交易). Non-firm offer is more flexible to the offeror as he can make decision of closing business according to the market situation. However, offerees often regard it as ordinary business dealings and pay little attention to it, which does no good to the conclusion of business.

✔ Lead In — Dialogues

Mr. Black (B) is at Mr. Anderson's (A) office, continuing to discuss the transaction about machine tools.

A: Here is a price list you asked for yesterday, Mr. Black. Here you are. All our FOB prices are listed here. As I said, our prices are usually decided on the size of your order. Will you please tell the quantity you require so as to enable us to sort out the offers?

B: In that case, I'll just jot down the quantity I need for reference. We want to buy 20,000 sets of "Dragon" machine tool KS-109.

A: Great, thank you very much.

B: By the way, how long does it take you to deliver the goods?

A: Usually we deliver the goods within 30 days after receipt of the covering letters of credit.

B: Okay. Can I have your exact FOB Tianjin prices now?

A: Let me see. The best price we can give you is USD 120 per set, FOB Tianjin.

B: I have to say, your price is unrealistic. It is higher than those we can get elsewhere.

Situation 3 Negotiations and Consultations

A: You have to take quality into consideration.

B: This price is still on the high side even for goods of this quality. The price of Japanese goods is nearly 10% lower than yours. I wonder whether you can reduce your price to that level.

A: Well, in view of our future business, I'd like to make an offer to you like this: 20,000 sets of "Dragon" machine tool KS-109, at USD 115 per set, FOB Tianjin. This is the best we can do. I hope that you can think of it, Mr. Black. And this offer subject to our final confirmation.

B: Okay, thank you. I'll talk about it with our manager and give you a reply as soon as possible.

A: No problem. I hope we can conclude the transaction.

Performing

Text

Sample 1   A Non-Firm Offer

Dear Sirs,

We acknowledge with thanks the receipt of your letter dated September 21, in which you express your interest in our Haier Refrigerators.

At your request, we take pleasure in making you the following offer, subject to our final confirmation.

Commodity: Haier Refrigerators

Specification: CDY 198

Quantity: 1,000 sets

Color: half white, half red

Price: at USD 320 per set CIF Alexandria

Shipment: one month after receipt of L/C

Payment: by confirmed, irrevocable L/C in our favor payable by draft at sight to reach the sellers one month before shipment and remain valid for negotiation in China till the 15 days after shipment.

As you know, our stock is limited and the demand is great. Your early decision is necessary.

We anticipate your prompt reply.

Yours respectfully,

Sample 2 A Non-Firm Offer

Dear Mr. Law,

We are very pleased to receive your inquiry of 16th September and enclose our illustrated catalogue and price list giving the details you ask for. Also under separate cover, we are sending you some samples and feel confident that when you have examined them, you will agree that the goods are both excellent in quality and reasonable in price.

On regular purchases for quantities of not less than 100 dozen of individual items, we would allow you a discount of 2%. Payment is to be made by an irrevocable L/C in our favour, payable by draft at sight. Details of our prices and other trade terms are stated in the price list mentioned above. This offer is subject to our final confirmation.

We invite your attention to our other products such as table-cloths and table napkins, details of which you will find in the catalogue, and look forward to receiving your first order.

Yours sincerely,
Wang Jie
Manager of Export Department
Guangdong Textiles Import and Export Corporation

Sample 3 A Non-Firm Offer

Dear sirs,

We are in receipt of your letter dated October 22, and are willing to enter into business relations with you on the basis of equality and mutual benefit.

Enclosed please find some sample books you requested. We hope that they will help you in making your selection. We are pleased to make you a special offer, subject to our final confirmation, as follows:

Art. No.	Name of Commodity	Price
JB 126	All Wool Melton	USD 6.15/Y CIF New York
JE 128	All Wool Gabardine	USD 6.82/Y CIF New York

For your information, the minimum quantity for order is 12,000 yards. Shipment is to be made in three equal monthly installments beginning from December, 2005. Payment is by L/C at sight. Goods are packed in bales or in wooden cases at seller's option. We hope that the above will be acceptable to you and assure you of our best service at any time.

We are looking forward to your trial order.

Yours faithfully,

Situation 3 Negotiations and Consultations

Notes

1) acknowledge with thanks the receipt of …   收到……，谢谢
2) at one's request   据……的请求
3) take pleasure in doing sth.   乐意干某事
4) stock   n. 存货

   from stock   可供现货（supply sth. from stock）
   in stock   有现货（have sth. in stock）
   the complete stock   现货商品，整批货
   e.g. We have 50 tons in stock.
        我们有50吨的现货。

   subject to…   以……为准
   remain an offer open   报盘保持有效
   offer from stock/ have goods in stock   供现货/有现货
   without engagement   没有约束的
   in view of …   鉴于……，考虑到……
   quotation sheet   报价单
   make a firm offer   报实盘
   unless otherwise stated   除非另有约定
   in receipt of   收到某物
   enter into business relations   建立业务关系
   on the basis of equality and mutual benefit   在平等互利的基础上
   final confirmation   最终确认

Practicing

I. Translate the following expressions into Chinese.

make sb. an offer for sth.   final confirmation
entertain a counter-offer   in a position
excessive demand   a close substitute
close business   without engagement
remain an offer open   make a firm offer

II. Fill in the following blanks with proper prepositions.

1. We refer _____ your offer _____ May 23.
2. We are prepared to keep the offer open _____ 21th this month.

087

3. The letter of credit will opened _____ your favor.

4. We shall make a reduction _____ our price if you increase your quantity _____ 4,000 pieces.

5. This offer is firm subject _____ your reply reaching us before May 10.

6. Please quote your lowest prices _____ FOB Tianjin.

7. We are prepared to place an order _____ you _____ 10,000 cases of Qingdao Beer.

8. We hope you will agree _____ our proposal and we look forward to receiving regular orders _____ you.

III. Translate the following sentences into English.

1. 感谢你方 5 月 15 日的询盘，现另邮寄上皮鞋样品及价目单。

2. 我方报盘以货物未售出为准。

3. 对于你方所要求的产品，我方报盘如下。

4. 对该产品的需求增大导致价格上涨。

5. 我们的报价是每套茶壶 500 元人民币，上海离岸价。

IV. Writing practice.

1. Write a non-firm offer to reply the enquiry given below.

Dear sirs,

　　We have seen your advertisement in today's "Times" and we are interested in your leather shoes for children.

　　Could you please send us your latest catalogue and price list? State your terms of payment and a trade discount for companies that buy in fairly large quantities.

　　If the prices are reasonable, we'll place regular orders for fairly large numbers.

Yours truly,

2. Write a letter about non-firm offer (open).

Supplement

✓ Supplementary Reading

1. Letter

Dear sirs,

　　We thank you for your enquiry of January 2. We are sorry to inform you that we are not in a position to offer you the desired goods, owing to excessive demand.

However, we would like to take this opportunity to offer without engagement the following products as a close substitute for your consideration: 300 sets of teapots No. 5230 at USD 30 per set, FOB Shanghai.

A sample is sent to you for your reference. And if you are able to close business as we propose here, please tell us ASAP.

Yours faithfully,

2. Reading

Unlike a firm offer, a non-firm offer is not binding upon the sellers. In other words, a non-firm offer can be withdrawn or changed by the sellers.

Non-firm offer is an informal offer made by the offeror, which has got no validity terms but with clear indication of its confirmation conditions, such as "subject to our final confirmation". It can be considered as an offer which are not upon binding the sellers and the details of the offers may change in certain situations.

Difference between a Firm Offer and a Non-Firm Offer

A firm offer is the offer with a certain time limit while a non-firm offer is the offer without engagement.

When a Non-Firm Offer Lapses?

For the non-firm offer, it isn't protected by the law. They have no lapses or not, only tell you I want to sell or buy something.

Major Features of Firm-Offer

1) The offer must be written clearly that the offer is firm.
2) The offer must be clear, definite, complete and final.
3) The offer must state the time of validity.
4) The offeror is free from any obligations.

✓ Knowledge Link

☆ 实盘与虚盘

实盘是发盘人（offeror）按其提供的条件以达成交易为目的的明确表示。实盘具有法律效应。受盘人（offeree）一旦在有效期内接受实盘上的条件和内容，发盘人就无权拒绝售货。一项实盘必须具备：

1. 发盘的内容和词句必须肯定，不能用"大约（about）""参考价（reference price）"等模棱两可的词。

2. 发盘的内容必须明确完整，其内容应包括商品品质（quality）、数量（quantity）、包装（packing）、价格（price）、装运（shipment）、支付（payment）和有效期（validity）等。

3. 发盘中不能有保留条件，如：以我方最后确认为准（subject to our final confirmation）；以货物未售出为准（subject to goods being unsold）。

虚盘是发盘人所做的不肯定交易的表示。凡不符合实盘所具备的上述三个条件的发盘，都是虚盘。虚盘无须详细的内容和具体条件，也不注明有效期，它仅表示交易的意向，不具有法律效应。

Task 5 Counter-Offer

Preparing

Relative Reading

What is Counter-Offer?

A counter-offer is an expression by the offeree of his disagreement, either in part or as a whole, to the offer made by the offeror.

A reply to an offer which purports to be an acceptance but contains additions, limitations or other modifications is a rejection of the offer and constitutes a counter-offer.

- Price, payment, quality and quantity of the goods
- Place and time of delivery
- Extent of one party's liability to the other
- The settlement of disputes

An offer made in response to a previous offer by the other party during negotiations for a final contract. Making a counter offer automatically rejects the prior offer, and requires an acceptance under the terms of the counter offer or there is no contract. Example: Susan Seller offers to sell her house for USD 150,000, to be paid in 60 days; Bruce Buyer receives the offer and gives Seller a counter offer of USD 140,000, payable in 45 days. The original offer is dead, despite the shorter time for payment since the price is lower. Seller then can choose to accept at USD 140,000, counter again at some compromise price, reject the counter offer, or let it expire.

Situation 3 Negotiations and Consultations

A Counter-Offer Includes the Following Parts

1) Thanks for the original offer;

2) Polite expressions of regret at the inability to accept the offer and the reasons to support it;

3) Suggestions or amendments to the original offer;

4) Hopes for acceptance of the changes and a quick reply.

How to Write a Counter-Offer?

An expression of thanks for an offer.

Regret to be unable to accept the offer and state reasons.

Make a counter-offer or suggest other opportunity to do business together.

Hope for early reply.

✔ Lead In — Dialogues

Mr. David Kinch (A), the general manager of Far East Industrial Corporation of America, are bargaining with Mr. Yu Ming (B) about the price.

A: Well, what do you think about our offer?

B: To be honest, your prices are still on a high side though you have adjusted. It would not be easy for us to push the sales if we buy it at this price.

A: If you can order more, we would like to make a further concession.

B: Order more? I'm afraid this can't be done unless you propose something definite together with larger improvement on your price.

A: If you order 2,000 sets, we are prepared to make another 3% reduction.

B: Well, let me consider. If you reduce your price by another 3%, we'll order 2,000 sets.

A: Do you mean that if the unit price of our computer is $810 per set, you'll order 2,000 sets?

B: Yes, I mean to say so.

A: Well, in order to make a quick turnover by reducing prices, we accept your conditions.

B: Thank you for making a concession in price once again, Mr. Kinch. The settlement of the price is the prelude of the success of the transaction. We might say that the success of this transaction is in sight.

A: We can confirm your order: 2,000 sets of COMPAQ 1200 computers, USD 810 CIF Shanghai. I hope there will be more business to come between us in the future.

Performing

Text

Sample 1 A Counter-Offer for Price Reduction

Dear Sirs,

We have received your letter of July 26, 2010, offering us 3,000 metric tons of groundnuts at CNY 1,800 net per metric ton CFR Singapore.

In reply, we regret to state that our end-users here find your price too high and out of line with the prevailing market level. Information indicates that the price of your products is 10% higher than that of the Japan origin.

To step up the trade, on behalf of our end-users, we counter-offer as follows, subject to your confirmation reaching us before the end of this week.

It is in view of our long-standing business relationship that we make you such counter-offer at CNY 1,600 net per metric ton CFR Singapore, other terms as per your letter of July 26.

We hope you will consider our counter-offer and inform us acceptance at your earliest convenience.

Yours respectfully,

Sample 2 Reply to the Above

Dear Sirs,

Thank you for letter of July 28, 2010. We are disappointed to hear that our price for groundnut is too high for you to work on. You mentioned that Japanese goods are being offered at a price approximately 10% lower than that quoted by us.

We accept what you say, but we are of the opinion that the quality of the other makes does not measure up to that of our products.

Although we are keen to do business with you, we regret that we cannot accept your counter-offer or even meet you half way. The best we can do is to reduce our previous quotation by 3%. We trust that this will meet with your approval.

We look forward to hearing from you.

Yours sincerely,

Sample 3　A Counter Offer

Dear Sirs,

Re: Your Offer of 100% Cashmere Sweaters

Thank you for your letter of April 7, in which you offered us 100% Cashmere Sweaters.

Regrettably, we are unable to accept your offer as your prices are too high. We operate on small margins. It means heavy loss to us to accept your prices. We also have similar offers from Korean make. They are 25% lower than yours.

We like the quality and design of your products. We accept that the quality of your products is better, but it does not justify such a large difference in price. We might do business with you if you could make us some allowance, say 20%, on your prices. Otherwise we have to decline your offer.

We hope you will consider our counter offer most favorably and let us have your reply soon.

Yours faithfully
A & D Supermarket

Notes

1) end-user　*n.* 客户，消费者
2) out of line with the prevailing market level　与现行市场价格不一致
3) Information indicates that...　消息表明，迹象表明

   类似的表达还有：

   Information shows that...

   Information states that...

   e. g. Information indicates that the value of the dollar declines because of the influence of the financial market.

   有消息表明，美元的价值受到金融市场的影响而下跌。

4) on behalf of　代表
5) at your earliest convenience　as soon as possible　尽早
6) work on　开展，进行下去

   e. g. We regret to say that the price you quoted is too high to work on.

   很遗憾，你方所报价格太高，无法进行下去。

7) be of the opinion　相信，坚信
8) measure up to　达到……标准
9) meet sb. half way　各让一半，折中处理

e. g. Shall we meet each other half way?

我们折中处理好么？

10) approval   *n.* 批准，同意

e. g. We will do our best to obtain the approval of the import license.

我们会尽力取得进口许可证的。

Practicing

I. Translate the following expressions into English.

还盘   谢绝还盘

同类产品   鉴于

价格偏高   折中处理

满足需求   达到……标准

各让一半，折中处理   与现行市场价格不一致

II. Fill in the blanks with proper forms of given words.

1. reduce

1) Buyers ask for a _____ in price.

2) In order to close this deal we shall further _____ our price.

3) Our closely calculated price cannot be further _____.

2. regret

1) It is _____ to decline your counter-offer, however, we can not but do so.

2) We are _____ that we did not advise you earlier.

3) We _____ to say that the quality does not measure up to the contracted standard.

3. approval

1) We have tried our best to meet with your _____ in this business.

2) Your request has been _____ of after our discussion.

3) We _____ of the fact that the price of raw material is declining, so our quotation will be slightly reduced.

4. handle

1) To give you a general idea of our products, we enclose a complete set of leaflets showing various products being _____ by this corporation.

2) What items do you mainly _____?

3) We are the leading importer of electronics in Lagos, mainly _____ the import of the electronic goods.

III. Translate the following sentences into English.

1. 如果你方能在报价上减少2%，我们将立即接受。
2. 很遗憾我们不能把价格降到你方所要求的水平。
3. 相同质量产品的价格相比，我们的价格总是偏低。
4. 如果订单在100打以上，我们愿意给予5%的折扣。
5. 鉴于长期的贸易关系，我们可以考虑减价3%。

IV. Writing practice.

Write a Letter about Counter-Offer According to the Following

1) Mr. Black has received your offer for black tea. He e-mailed you to make a counter-offer and showed his reasons. Please write a letter of making a counter-offer.

2) Mr. Zhang has received Jinxing Company's offer for wool blankets. Mr. Zhang e-mailed the company to make a counter-offer and showed his reasons. Please write a letter of making a counter-offer.

Supplement

✓ Supplementary Reading

1. Letter 1: Buyer Asking for Reduction of Minimum Quantity

Dear sirs,

We thank you for your fax of April 19 offering us 6 designs of Ornamental Cloth. However, we regret to inform you that the minimum of 10,000 yards per design is too big for this market.

In case you reduce the minimum to 7,000 yards per design, there is a possibility of placing orders with you, because a considerable quantity of this material is required on this market for manufacturing curtains, bed sheets, etc.

Your early reply will be highly appreciated.

Yours faithfully,

2. Letter 2: Buyer Asking for Earlier Delivery

Dear sirs,

DELL PC

We refer to your offer of August 10 for 2,000 sets of the subject articles.

As our customer urgently need the goods, they request us to fax you to shift the delivery

time from "October, 2010" to "on or before September 15, 2010", or they will get the goods from other resources.

In order to promote your business, please accept this un-harsh condition.

We await your pleasant reply.

Yours sincerely,

3. Reading: Counter-Counter-Offer（反还盘）

A reply of the offeror to the counter-offer of the offeree.

There're always several rounds of offer, counter-offer, counter-counter-offer, till business is finalized or called off.

Should write a counter-counter-offer with good care and with a view to goodwill and try to convince the other side and encourage the business.

4. Letter 3: Specimen Letter

Dear Sirs,

Re: Your counter offer of our 100% Cashmere Sweaters

Thank you for your letter of April 22. We are sorry to learn you find our prices too high.

Although we would like to do business with you, we are very sorry that we are unable to entertain your counter-offer.

Our prices are carefully calculated. We have even taken quantity orders into consideration. We have to point out that we have received a lot of orders from other buyers, which shows that our prices are reasonable.

At present, the market for 100% Cashmere Sweaters is strong with upward tendency. It is not likely that any significant change will take place in the foreseeable future. It is in your interest to place an order with us as soon as you can.

We also have Cashmere Sweaters, 50% cashmere / 50% wool. They are of the same design but much cheaper than 100% Cashmere Sweaters.

We are enclosing our price list for such sweaters. If you are interested, please let us know.

We are looking forward to receiving an order from you.

Yours faithfully
China National Import and Export Corporation

 Knowledge Link

☆ 还盘函的撰写要求

受盘人不同意发盘中的交易条件而提出修改或变更的意见，称为还盘（counter-offer）。

报盘人发盘后，受盘人往往会进行还盘。发盘人收到对方的还盘后，通常要做出接受或拒绝的答复，也可以进行再还盘。

还盘函的撰写应当做到数字准确，叙述清楚，不能因为需要从对方角度考虑措辞而将本意的"不同意"写得模棱两可。

Sum-Up

The following are sentences usually used in business negotiation by letters (enquiry, offer and counter-offer).

1. Making an Enquiry

◇ We are interested in your... and wishes to have your quotations for...

我们对贵方产品……很感兴趣，请就……报价。

◇ One of our clients takes interest in your... and we should be glad if you give us the terms of the item.

我们的一位顾客对贵方的……很感兴趣，如你方能给我方关于这项商品的条件，我们将不胜感激。

◇ Will you please send us your catalogue together with detailed offer?

请寄目录并附带详细报价。

◇ In order to promote business between us, we are sending you samples and price lists, under separate cover, for your reference.

为促进双方业务往来，另封寄上样品以供参考。

2. Making an Offer

◇ Thank you for your enquiry of... and we are pleased to quote as follows:

感谢贵方……的询盘，现报盘如下：

◇ With reference to your enquiry, we make you a firm offer...

兹提及你方询盘，我们报实盘如下：

◇ We are making you an offer of..., subject to our final confirmation.

兹报盘……，以我方最后确认为有效。

◇ We will keep our offer firm to the end of this month.

我们将此盘有效期保留至本月底。

3. Accepting an Offer

◇ We have received your offer of... which is acceptable to us.

我方收到你方……的报盘，所有条款均可接受。

◇ We would like to conclude business on the terms in your letter dated...

愿与你方按你方……信中所提条款成交。

◇ If the above is acceptable to you, we can place a large order.
如果上述条款你方能接受，我们将大量订购。

4. Making a Counter-Offer

◇ We regret to tell you that your price is on the high side.
很遗憾告知，你方价格偏高。

◇ We counteroffer as follows.
我方还盘如下。

◇ Accepting your offer will leave us with only a small profit.
接受你方的报盘意味着我方将无利可图。

◇ This is our rock-bottom price, we can't make you any further reduction.
这是我方的最低价格，我们不能再降价了。

Situation 04: Conclusion of Business and the Fulfillment of a Contract

Objectives

1) To be able to properly translate and write an order, and acknowledge the letters with orders enclosed.

2) To be able to translate and write letters to express the orders received have been accepted or rejected.

3) To be able to make out contracts and write letters to send contracts.

Introduction

Orders and Their Contents

An order is a request to supply a specified quantity of goods. Usually, an order is a symbol of acceptance, but it can be used as a buying offer, an acceptance or a confirmation. An order may be given by a printed order form, letter, fax, e-mail, etc. When writing an order letter, you must include all the specifics necessary to complete the order to your satisfaction. Usually, your letter should include information about the following matters:

1) A full description of the commodity, including model number, size, color, or any other relevant information.

2) Quantity.

3) Date and method of shipment.

4) Price per item.

5) Packing.

6) Payment.

Contracts and Their Contents

After a firm offer is accepted or an acceptance is confirmed, usually the sellers will make out a contract or a sales confirmation. A sales contract or a sales confirmation (S/C) will go into effect immediately upon signature.

In a letter sending a contract, the following contents should be included.

1) Confirming the business agreement.

2) Stating that you have enclosed a contract confirmation.

3) Requesting the return of one copy duly signed for your file.

4) Expressing your expectation of the counter-signature, promise or hope for future business.

Task 1 Orders and Acknowledgement

Preparing

Relative Reading

What Is an Order?

When users pay for the products that they purchase from your web site, Commerce Server 2009 creates an order. An order can contain a variety of information. For example, an order can contain line item information, an order sub total, shipping, discount, tax information, and total order cost. An order can also contain customers' information, such as customers' name and address, currency used, the date the order was placed or last modified, and extended data about the order.

By using the Customer and Orders Manager, you can view orders that were placed on your web site. You can delete orders if you have the required permissions. To change your Customer and Orders Manager permissions, see your site developer.

By using Commerce Server 2009, you can exchange orders with other order processing systems. Site developers can use the BizTalk Server adapters that Commerce Server 2009 provides to integrate other order processing systems with Commerce Server 2009. For more information about adapters, see "Developing with the BizTalk Adapters" in Commerce Server 2009 Help.

Different Samples of Order Letters

Order

Placing an Order

Situation 4 Conclusion of Business and the Fulfillment of a Contract

Repeat an Order

Reply

Acceptance

Declining

Requirement for Order Writing

1) Thanks for the seller.

2) Express you are preparing to place an order with the seller.

3) Require an accurate and full description of goods.

a. Name \ specification \ art Nos. \ size.

b. Quantity, prices including unit and total.

c. Packing \ shipping marks.

d. Date and method of shipping.

e. Terms of payment.

4) The buyer's name and the seller's name should be clearly written in the order.

5) An order number must be included.

6) Express your desire for future business.

✓ Lead In — Dialogues

Lisa: We love your products, and would like to place an order with you as soon as possible.

Bob: Well, I'm afraid we can't proceed with the order until the Christmas holiday. Our factories will be closed for another week.

Lisa: That's all right. We will send you a purchase order in one week. I hope you will take care of it.

Bob: Sure. Once we get your purchase order, we will begin the execution of the order right away.

Lisa: Many thanks. We need the products in less than one month, because we have a big deal with another company.

Bob: That will be fine. And I can promise you that you will get the goods about two weeks after we get your purchase order.

Performing

✓ Text

Sample 1 Sending an Order

Dear Sir or Madam,

Thank you very much for your letter of June 15, 2011 with models and price lists. We have chosen Article No. 1338 for which we enclose order No. 988. The goods are urgently required, so prompt delivery will be most appreciated.

We hope this order is workable to you and look forward to your earliest reply.

Yours sincerely,
Zhu Kai

Sample 2　Reply to the Order

Dear Sir,

Thank you very much for your order of June 16 for Article No. 1338. We will make every possible effort to speed up delivery. We will advise you of the date of dispatch. We are at your service at all times.

Sincerely,
Bob

Sample 3　Sending a Purchase Order

Dear Sirs,

Re: Brand Name Shoes

We enclose our Order AC 502 for the three items in your latest catalogue.

We learn that these goods can be shipped from stock and wish you to send them without delay. Looking forward to your sales confirmation.

Yours sincerely,
Zhang Lan

Notes

1) price list　价目表
2) prompt delivery　尽快交货
   prompt　*adj.*　迅速的，即时的
   delivery　*n.*　递送，交货
3) appreciate　*v.*　感激
   e. g. I appreciate your help. / Your help is appreciated.
   　　　　我感谢你的帮助。
4) workable　*adj.*　可经营的，可使用的，可行的
5) make an effort to do　努力
   make every possible effort to do　尽全力
6) speed up　加速

Situation 4 Conclusion of Business and the Fulfillment of a Contract

7) advise   *v.* 报告，通知

　　advise sb. of   把……报告（通知）某人

8) dispatch   *n.* 派遣；发送

9) at your service   听您吩咐；随时供您使用

10) at all times   总是

Practicing

I. Translate the following expressions into Chinese.

price list   prompt delivery
appreciate   workable
make an effort to do   speed up
advise sb. of   at your service
looking forward   sales confirmation

II. Translate the following sentences into Chinese.

1. We confirm herewith your telegraphic order of the 10th June, for 100 cwt. of the best sugar.

2. We acknowledge receipt of your favor of the 10th July, and thank you for the order you have given us.

3. We received your letter of the 10th inst., and thank you for your order for children's jackets.

4. We are in receipt of your favour of the 10th May, with your order for five printing machines, which I herewith acknowledge with best thanks.

5. We'd like to place a trial order for a small amount of the new varieties.

III. Fill in the following blanks with the suitable words given below.

| of   following   in   confirm   irrevocable   medium |

Gentlemen:

The price contained in your e-mail _____ May 20, 2002 gained favorable attention with us.

We would like to order the _____ items consisting of various colors, patterns and assortments:

Large 2,000 dozen

_____ 4,000 dozen

Small 2,000 dozen

As the sales season is approaching, the total order quantity should be shipped in July.

At that time an _____ L/C for the total purchase value will be opened.

Please _____ the order and E-mail a shipping schedule.

Sincerely,

IV. Writing Practice

1. Writing a letter stating the following points.

   1) You have received their Order No. 102.

   2) Express your thanks to them.

   3) You will ship the goods duly.

   4) Hope a future cooperation.

2. Write a letter about placing an order.

Supplement

 Supplementary Reading

1. A Reply to an Order Letter

Dear Sir or Madam:

We are pleased to receive your order of September 5, 2007 for Shanghai Printed Pure Silk and welcome you as one of our customers.

We confirm the supply of Shanghai Printed Pure Silk at the prices stated in your letter as follows (All the prices are CIF San Francisco.):

Pattern Number	Unit Prices	Total Amount	Quantity
9001	USD 12 per yd.	USD 180,000	15,000 yards
9003	USD 15 per yd.	USD 150,000	10,000 yards

We are arranging for dispatch next week on S. S. "Dongfeng". When the goods reach you, we feel confident that you will be completely satisfied with them.

As you may not be aware of the wide range of goods we deal in, we are enclosing a copy of our catalogue and hope that our handling of your first order with us will lead to further business between us and mark the beginning of positive working relationship.

Yours sincerely,

Situation 4　Conclusion of Business and the Fulfillment of a Contract

2. Placing an Order

Placing an order means that the buyer is going to order the needed goods according to the transaction terms accepted by both parties after repeated negotiation.

3. Types

There are two types of orders. If it is the first time of you to close a deal with your supplier, the order is called an initial order; otherwise, it is called a repeated order.

4. How to Place an Order?

Placing orders through your local distributors.

Placing your order on line directly.

Phone & fax order.

Placing an order by e-mail.

Mail order.

5. An Order

Specification and description of the commodity indicates the name of the product, the model or article numbers, the page of the catalog from which you are ordering, names and addresses of both parties, even their telex numbers.

6. Order Form

Info of Buyer

Order No.

Date

Info of Seller

Description of Order

Packing

Shipment

Terms of Payment

7. Acknowledgement

Expression of thanks or pleasures for receiving the order.

Assurance of immediate actions for fulfilling the order.

Introduction to the other lines of products produced. Arouse the buyer's attention to other products of the company to expand the future business.

Expectation for future orders. Encourage the buyer to order more products.

8. Some Printed Routine Acknowledgment

Acknowledgement for 2,000 Sets of Full-Automatic Washing Machine

Acknowledgement for 3 M/Ts of Walnut

Acknowledgement of Equipment

 Knowledge Link

☆ 外贸订单如何承接？

外贸订单的承接一直是困扰从事外贸工作的新人的疑难问题，其实承接外贸订单无外乎做到四个合适条件：合适的时间；合适的方式；合适的客户；合适的贸易条件。结合客观条件，再加之方法、积累、努力、智慧、韧性等，有效地利用，实践加总结，必然达到外贸订单承接的游刃有余的境界。

外贸订单的质与量必须依靠于外贸公司的经验和决断力。因为外贸订单的承接，表面上似是纯粹的业务问题，实际上却是企业应对困难和危机的一种综合能力。与此同时，外贸订单的质与量在于外贸公司的实力、积累和策略等综合环节，只有很好地了解、协调、开展才能获得优质、数量化的外贸订单。

Task 2 Acceptance or Rejection of Orders

Preparing

 Relative Reading

Acceptance and Confirmation

An acceptance is a fact that the buyers or sellers agree completely to all the terms and conditions in an offer (or a counter-offer as a new offer). If the offer is a firm offer, a deal is concluded after acceptance. If the offer is a non-firm offer, a deal is not concluded until the acceptance is confirmed by the buyers or sellers. In a letter for acceptance or conformation, all the necessary terms and conditions may need a further confirmation/check from both sides.

A mirror model, which means, unconditional acceptance, without any discrepancies between what is offered and what is accepted, otherwise it is a counter offer. No material alterations are allowed nowadays by legal experts.

Situation 4 Conclusion of Business and the Fulfillment of a Contract

Structure of Acceptance

1) Confirmation/acknowledgement/gratitude
2) Indicate acceptance
3) Draw attention to other goods
4) Expectations

Rules for Making Acceptances

(1) Be Cautious

Because once an acceptance has been made and has arrived at the offerer, it means the formation of a contract. Both the offeror and offferee have to be legally bound by the contract.

(2) Pay More Attention to the Date of Expiry

Acceptance should be made before the expiry date of the offer, otherwise it is ineffective, unless the offerer accepts it right away or in a reasonable period of time. The reply to a counter-offer also constitutes an acceptance, so it has to follow relevant rules discussed in this unit.

(3) Acceptance Unconditionally

Do not make any alterations in the trade terms stipulated in the offer, otherwise it is a counter-offer.

(4) Withdraw the Acceptance in Time, If Necessary

The letter of withdrawing should reach the offerer before the acceptance arrives, otherwise the acceptance has come into effect. The contractual relationship has be legally established.

Rejection or Offering Substitute

If the terms and conditions in the order are not satisfactory, it is impossible for the seller to accept, then the seller may reject the order.

In rejecting the order, it must be written with great care: goodwill, simple, polite and considerate.

Sometimes the goods may run out of stock or due to some other reasons, the seller may offer substitutes.

✓ Lead In — Dialogues

Bob: How about 15% for the first six months, and for the second six months at 12%, with a guarantee of 3,000 units?

Lisa: In that case, we only gain very low profit margins.

Bob: It's about the best we can do, Lisa. We need to hammer something out today. If I go back empty-handed, I might be coming back to you soon to ask for a job.

Lisa: OK, 17% for the first six months, 14% for the second?

Bob: Good. Let's iron out the remaining details. When do you want to take delivery?

Lisa: We'd like you to execute the first order by the 31st.

Bob: Let me run through this again: the first shipment for 1,500 units, to be delivered in 27 days, by the 31st.

Lisa: Right. We cannot handle much larger shipments.

Bob: Fine. But I'd prefer the first shipment to be 1,000 units, then 2,000 units. The 31st is quite soon — I can't guarantee 1,500 units.

Lisa: I can agree to that. Well, if there's nothing else, I think we've settled everything.

Bob: Lisa, this deal promises big returns for both sides. Let's hope it's the beginning of a long and prosperous relationship.

Performing

Text

Sample 1   Accepting an Order

Dear Mike,

We acknowledge with thanks your letter of June 2, together with your valued Order No. 101. We will expedite your order immediately and we assure you that the goods will be forwarded within the coming month. We hope you will be satisfied with both the goods and our arrangements.

                                                    Yours sincerely,
                                                    Lily

Sample 2   Rejecting an Order

Dear Mike,

We thank you for your Order No. 101 for delivery in July.

We regret, however, that we cannot book the order at the prices we quoted six weeks ago. As you know, freight and the cost of materials have risen substantially in the meantime, and we were compelled to adjust our prices in order to cover at least part of this increase.

The lowest prices we can quote today are as follows:

Situation 4　Conclusion of Business and the Fulfillment of a Contract

"Ome" Shampoo at USD 50 per dozen. "Ome" Toilet Soap at USD 36 per dozen.

The above prices are understood on CIF Singapore basis. Please inform us by return whether we may book your order at these revised prices; we shall then be able to give you delivery in July as required.

Yours faithfully,
Lily

Sample 3　Letter of Rejection

Dear Miss Liyun,

Your order No. 93120

Thank you for your Order No. 93120 for 1,000 sets of "RuYi" Brand Color TV, but since you make delivery before Christmas as a firm condition, we deeply regret that we cannot supply you at present.

The manufacturers are finding it impossible to meet current demand for their stock is exhausted but consecutive new orders are pouring in. Though the workers are speeding up the production, the buyers still have to wait. Another client of us placed, through us, an order for 500 sets a month ago, and is informed that his order could not be dealt with until the beginning of February next year.

We are sorry that we cannot meet your requirement this time. But if you are interested in other brands, please let us know.

Yours faithfully,
Gao Jing

Notes

1) acknowledge　*v.* 告知收到，确认收悉

　　e.g. We acknowledge with thanks your letter of June 2.

　　贵方六月二日来信收悉，十分感谢。

2) valued　*adj.* 贵重的，尊贵的，宝贵的

　　此处用来修饰 order，表示对对方的尊重，体现出商务函电 courtesy（礼貌）的特点。
　　类似的表达还有 valuable　*adj.* 贵重的，有价值的，颇有价值的。

3) expedite　*v.* 加快，加速

　　e.g. The builders promised to expedite the repairs.

　　建筑商答应加速修理。

4) assure　*v.* 保证，担保

assure sb. of sth.　　使某人确信某事

assure sb. that ...　向某人保证……

　　e. g. I can assure you of the reliability of the news.

　　　　我可以向你保证这消息是可靠的。

5) forward　v. 转寄，运送

　　e. g. We are forwarding you our catalogue.

　　　　我们把我们的目录寄给你。

6) regret　v. &n. 遗憾，后悔

　　表示遗憾的表达有：I regret (to say) that...我很遗憾……；很抱歉……；

　　It is to be regretted that ...使人遗憾的是……；真可惜……；

　　Much to my regret, ……非常遗憾。

　　e. g. Much to my regret, I'm unable to accept your kind invitation.

　　　　我不能接受你盛情的邀请，非常遗憾。

7) book an order　接受订单

　　book　v. 登记，注册

8) quote　v. 开价；报价

　　quote sb. a price for sth.

　　e. g. Please quote us the price for 34 inch color TV sets.

　　　　请向我方报34寸彩电价格。

　　quotation　n. 报价

9) as follows　如下

　　注意：此短语在使用时 follow 后的 s 不能省去。

　　e. g. We quote the prices as follows.

　　　　我方报价如下。

10) as required　依照请求

　　相似的表达还有：at your request

Practicing

I. Translate the following expressions into Chinese.

acknowledge	assure sb.
forward	It is to be regretted that ...
book/accept an order	quote sb. a price for sth.
as follows	as required
at your request	kind invitation

Situation 4 Conclusion of Business and the Fulfillment of a Contract

II. Translate the following sentences into Chinese.

1. To our regret, owing to shortage of stocks, we are unable to accept your Order No. 702.

2. We regret to inform you that we have to delay the delivery date because of shipment.

3. As for large need for order, the products delivered in the end of the year have been sold out.

4. We assure you that any further enquiries from you will receive our prompt attention.

5. We confirm having purchased from you 7,000 tons of cement on the following terms and conditions.

III. Translate the following Chinese into English.

1. 我已接受你方85号订单订购货号002号印花布10万码。

2. 你公司7月14日来函内附1,000台缝纫机订单已收到。

3. 我方很高兴接受你方6月14日报盘,请寄销售合同确认书一式两份,以便存档。

4. 为避免与本地海关发生摩擦,请你方仔细阅读装货说明。

5. 我们确认已向贵方按下列条件购买7,000吨水泥。

IV. Writing practice

1. Translate the following letter.

Letter 1

我们今早接到贵方222号订单,定购8,000打棉质衬衫,十分感谢。但可能要使贵方失望了,十分抱歉。

目前我们没有贵方所需尺寸的衬衫存货,而且至少在5个星期内亦不会有货。在此期间贵方可从别处购买衬衫,如未能购到,一旦新货运到,我们定当立即通知贵方。

Letter 2

Thank you for your enquiry of 25th August. We are always pleased to hear from a valued customer. I regret to say that we cannot agree to your request for technical information regarding our software security systems. The fact is, that most of our competitors also keep such information private and confidential. I sincerely hope that this does not inconvenience you in any way. If there is any other way in which we can help, do not hesitate to contact us again.

2. Writing a letter about accepting an order.

3. Write a letter about rejecting an order.

4. Write a letter about reluctantly accepting an order.

Supplement

Supplementary Reading

1. Letters of Regret

1) Rejecting Ordered Price

refer to

bid

rough weather

at economic prices

with an upward/ a downward tendency

2) Rejection for the Reason of No Supply

stock

revert to

come up

come to terms

come to deal

come to business

strike the deal

clinch the deal

ink the deal

strike hands

strike the bargain/the deal

close the bargain/the deal

put the deal through

give one's hands on bargain

3) Expressions Used When Freely Accepting an Offer

Come to think of it…

If you insist …

I'm sold…

In that case…

Now that you mention it…

On second thought…

That's an offer I can't refuse!

Situation 4   Conclusion of Business and the Fulfillment of a Contract

You've sold me!

You've talked me into it.

When you put in that way…

4) Expressions Used When Reluctantly Accepting an Offer

Given that there seems to be no other choice…

If I absolutely have to…

If that's the only alternative…

If that's the only way…

If that's the way it's got to be…

If there's no other alternative…

If there's no other way…

If you insist…

Okay, just this once.

That's an offer I guess I'd better not refuse!

Well, under those circumstances…

5) Expressions Used to Strengthen Arguments

Along with that…

And another thing…

And I might add…

Besides…

Furthermore…

In addition to that…

Moreover…

Not only that, but…

Not to mention the fact that…

Plus the fact that…

What's more…

6) Expressions Used When Giving In

If you really insist.

(I guess) You're right (after all).

(I guess) You've convinced me.

I'll buy that.

I'll go along with that.

I'm sold.

Maybe you're right.

Perhaps in this case (you're right).

You may have a point there. (You've got a point there.)

You've sold me.

2. Useful Expressions

We accept your firm offer.

We have accepted your firm offer.

We are accepting your offer.

We accept your offer subject to December Shipment.

3. 外贸拒绝订单函电的常用例句

1) Unfortunately, the goods you requested cannot be supplied from stock due to heavy commitments.

   很遗憾,由于订单堆积,您要的货物无现货可供。

2) The present supplies of raw materials are being used for earlier orders, which makes it impossible for us to effect your shipment as required.

   目前供应的原料正用于早期的订货,这使我们无法按你方要求交货。

3) We find it difficult to fill your order at the prices indicated in your letter because of the high cost of raw materials.

   由于原料成本高昂,我们难以按你方要求的价格供货。

4) We have to delay your order until the revised one reached the minimum volume we have established.

   只有你方把现有订货量增至我们所确定的最低数量,我们才能供货。

5) The immediate shipment of your order can be expected only when you modify your usual delivery arrangements by shipping 40% in June and balance in July instead of two equal monthly shipments.

   假如你方能把原来六、七月各装运一半改为六月运40%,其余的七月运,我们才有望立刻发货。

 Knowledge Link

☆ 接订单的五大技巧

1. 直接请求法

这是最有效、最直接地获取订单的方法,一般在销售员接到客户购买信号后,用明确的语言向客户直接提出购买建议(购买选择)。这种方法能够快速地帮助客户做出购买选择,节省

Situation 4 Conclusion of Business and the Fulfillment of a Contract

销售时间，提高工作效率。一般在以下三种情况下，这种方法都会成功：第一，销售沟通中客户未提出异议，对销售员的销售介绍没有反对意见时，销售员可以直接提问：李经理，您看，如果没有什么问题，我们就签合同吧？第二，销售沟通过程中客户有异议，但是通过销售介绍这种担心消除了，而且对产品表现出很大的兴趣时，销售员可以直接提问：黄经理，您打算订多少货？第三，客户已有意购买，但不愿先开口，此时销售员可以直接提问：王经理，这个机器的运输与安装，我将亲自全程参加。我们今天把购买合同签好，可以吗？

2．利益总结法

销售员在销售对谈过程中客户都给予正面的回应。销售员就可以帮助客户综合销售对谈中提到的各种利益，以促使客户做出明智的决策。

3．平衡表法

平衡表法有时被称为本·富兰克林法。销售对谈过程中，客户对销售成交没有明显异议。销售员可以在一张普通的纸上画一个"T"，在纵线的每侧写一个标题，在下面留下空白，以便填写特定的利益和卖点，然后邀请客户一起列出购买决策的理由。

4．探究法

销售员用事先设计好的探究式问句来发现潜在客户犹豫不决的原因，一旦弄清楚了这些原因，销售员就问一些"如果……您愿意……"的提问。这个方法试图把潜在客户关心的问题都拿到桌面上来谈。当客户关心的问题识别出来后，销售员可以成功解决这些问题，销售员就可以获得订单。

5．选择法

销售员向潜在客户提供几种可供选择的购买方案，让客户自己做出选择。一般把产品的属性作为选择内容的提示物，诸如产品价格、规格、性能、订货数量、送货方式、时间和地点等。选定的范围不要超过三个。

Task 3 Sending Contracts

Preparing

Relative Reading

What Is a Contract?

A contract is a formal written agreement which sets forth rights and obligations of the parties concerned.

1) A binding agreement between two or more parties for performing, or refraining from performing, some specified acts in exchange for lawful consideration.

2) The unit of trade for a financial or commodity future, or a voluntary, deliberate, and legally binding agreement between two or more competent parties. Contracts are usually written but may be spoken or implied, and generally have to do with employment, sale or lease, or tenancy.

A contractual relationship is evidenced by:

a. An offer.

b. The acceptance of the offer.

c. A valid (legal and valuable) consideration.

Each party to a contract acquires rights and duties relative to the rights and duties of the other parties. However, while all parties may expect a fair benefit from the contract (otherwise courts may set it aside as inequitable), it does not follow that each party will benefit to an equal extent.

Types of Business Contracts

Form-Style Contract（结构式合同）

—The standard contract (printed in advance with some blanks left for future signature).

Clause-Style Contract（条款式合同）

—More complex and detailed (the terms and conditions are more concretely stated with substantial sub-clauses).

What Is the Importance of Contracts to a Business?

The business environment is full of agreements between businesses and individuals. While oral agreements can be used, most businesses use formal written contracts when engaging in operations. Written contracts provide individuals and businesses with a legal document stating the expectations of both parties and how negative situations will be resolved. Contracts also are legally enforceable in a court of law. Contracts represent a tool that companies use to safeguard their resources.

✓ Lead In — Dialogues

Lisa: We are so glad our cooperation has a good beginning.
Bob: Yeah, that's wonderful! We've got the contract ready for signature. These are two originals of the contract we prepared.
Lisa: Oh, it's very nice. Can I have a look?
Bob: Sure.

Situation 4 Conclusion of Business and the Fulfillment of a Contract

Lisa: May I refer you to the contract stipulation about commodity? You'd better state the description of the goods more exactly in the contract.

Bob: Fine, we will do it right now.

Lisa: We sincerely hope that the goods can be shipped on time.

Bob: I'm sure that shipment will be effected according to the contract stipulation.

Performing

Text

Sample 1 A Letter of Sending Contract

Dear Mike,

Thank you for your letter of July 30, 2007 confirming the order of 12,000 pcs of Children's jackets.

Enclosed is our signed S/C No. MH-FS008 in duplicate. Please kindly countersign them and return one copy for our file.

We assure you that we will try our best to execute the contract strictly conforming to the S/C stipulations. And we hope the goods will turn out to be satisfactory in your market. Please open the relative L/C in our favor immediately so that we can arrange shipment in time.

Best regards,

Sample 2 A Reply to the Letter of Sending Contract

Dear Lily,

We have received your letter of Aug. 2, 2007, together with the S/C No. MH-FS008 with many thanks.

Attached please find one counter-signed copy returned for your file. We will duly instruct our bank to open the relevant L/C.

Please make sure that the goods will be ready for shipment in due course and keep us informed of your execution of this contract. We hope this first transaction will turn out to our mutual satisfaction and facilitate our future cooperation.

With best wishes,

Sample 3 Signing a Contract

Dear Sir or Madam:

This is regarding our quotation dated 2 November, and our mail offer dated 8 November concerning the supply of widgets（小机具）. We are prepared to our offer open until the end of this month.

For your information, the market is firm and growing. There is very little likelihood of any significant change in the visible future. As this product is in great demand and the supply is limited. To secure your order, we should recommend that you accept this offer without delay.

Yours sincerely,
Hillary

Notes

1) confirm   v. 确认

   e. g. Please confirm your telephone message by writing to me.

   请给我来封信，好进一步证实你在电话中传达的消息。

   confirmation   n. 确认

   Sales Confirmation   销售确认书

2) Enclosed is …

   正常语序为…is enclosed，该处使用倒装语序是为了强调后面的内容。

3) in duplicate   一式两份

4) countersign   会签，确认签（一个已签文件），如为了使之生效

5) for our file   以供我们存档

   类似的结构还有：for your reference 供您参考

6) execute   v. 执行；实行

   e. g. The manager assistant came here to execute a few small commissions for the manager. 经理助理到这里来是代替经理办几件小事的。

7) conform to   符合，遵照

8) in one's favor   对某人有利，此处表示以某人为信用证的受益人。

9) Attached/Enclosed please find…   随函寄去……请查收！

   e. g. Enclosed please find a copy of our price list.

   随函寄去我方价目表一份，请查收！

10) duly   adv. 适当；合适；及时

    e. g. Your suggestion has been duly noted.

    你的建议受到了重视。

    in due course   及时的，在适当的时候

    keep us informed of   告知我方

    to our mutual satisfaction   让我们双方都满意

Situation 4 Conclusion of Business and the Fulfillment of a Contract

Practicing

I. Translate the following expressions into Chinese.

confirm to   in duplicate
countersign   for our file
in due course   in one's favor
keep us informed of   to our mutual satisfaction
open the relevant L/C   confirming the order

II. Translate the following phrases about contracts.

合同条款   合同规定
签合同   撤销合同
解除合同   生效
失效   执行合同
确认合同   销售确认书

III. Fill in the following blanks with the suitable words given below.

| appreciated | in | to | duplicate | countersign | open |

Dear Mr. Sims,

Referring _____ the faxes exchanged between us resulting _____ the conclusion of business for 200 tons of Oysters, we are enclosing our sales Contract No. 39 in _____. Please _____ and return the bottom copy to us for our file.

We trust you will _____ the necessary Letter of Credit as soon as possible.

Your quick answer will be _____.

              Sincerely yours,
              Alice,

IV. Writing practice.

1. Write a letter to Mr. Zhang stating the following points.
   1) You have received their sales Contract No. 101 sent on September 20, 2011.
   2) You have enclosed a signed copy of the contract.
   3) You have opened a L/C in their favor.
2. Write a letter about singing a contract (open).
3. Write a letter about replying to the above.

V. Translate the following into English.

1. 有关本合同买卖双方之间引起的任何纠纷,争议或分歧,均可付诸仲裁。仲裁应在中国举行，应按照中国的有关仲裁法规进行裁决。

2. 合同已于今日生效，我们不能反悔了。

3. 合同一经中国政府批准，对双方就有了法律约束力。

4. 我们不得不要求你们按合同办事。

5. 你们必须把他们的权益订在合同中。

6. 我们坚持重合同，守信用。

Supplement

Supplementary Reading

1. 销售合同范本

合同 CONTRACT

日期：Date：　　合同号码：Contract No.：

买方：(The Buyers)　　卖方：(The Sellers)

兹经买卖双方同意按照以下条款由买方购进、卖方售出以下商品：

This contract is made by and between the Buyers and the Sellers; whereby the Buyers agree to buy and the Sellers agree to sell the under-mentioned goods subject to the terms and conditions as stipulated hereinafter:

1) 商品名称 Name of Commodity

2) 数量 Quantity

3) 单价 Unit Price

4) 总值 Total Value

5) 包装 Packing

6) 生产国别 Country of Origin

7) 支付条款 Terms of Payment

8) 保险 Insurance

9) 装运期限 Time of Shipment

10) 起运港 Port of Lading

11) 目的港 Port of Destination

12) 索赔：在货到目的口岸45天内如发现货物品质、规格和数量与合同不附，除属保险公司或船方责任外，买方有权凭中国商检出具的检验证书或有关文件向卖方索赔换货或赔款。

Claims

Within 45 days after the arrival of the goods at the destination, should the quality, specifications or quantity be found not in conformity with the stipulations of the contract except those claims for which the insurance company or the owners of the vessel are liable, the Buyers shall, have the right on the strength of the inspection certificate issued by CCIC and the relative documents to claim for compensation to the Sellers.

13) 不可抗力:由于人力不可抗力的原因在制造、装载或运输的过程中导致卖方延期交货或不能交货者,卖方可免除责任。在不可抗力发生后,卖方须立即电告买方及在14天内以空邮方式向买方提供事故发生的证明文件,在上述情况下,卖方仍须负责采取措施尽快发货。

Force Majeure

The sellers shall not be held responsible for the delay in shipment or non-delivery of the goods due to Force Majeure, which might occur during the process of manufacturing or in the course of loading or transit. The sellers shall advise the Buyers immediately of the occurrence mentioned above within fourteen days. The Sellers shall send by airmail to the Buyers for their acceptance certificates of the accident. Under such circumstances, the Sellers, however, are still under the obligation to take all necessary measures to hasten the delivery of the goods.

14) 仲裁:凡有关执行合同所发生的一切争议应通过友好协商解决,如协商不能解决,则将分歧提交中国国际贸易促进委员会按有关仲裁程序进行仲裁。仲裁将是终局的,双方均受其约束,仲裁费用由败诉方承担。

Arbitration

All disputes in connection with the execution of this Contract shall be settled friendly through negotiation. In case no settlement can be reached, the case then may be submitted for arbitration to the Arbitration Commission of China Council for the Promotion of International Trade in accordance with the Provisional Rules of Procedure promulgated by the said Arbitration Commission. The Arbitration committee shall be final and binding upon both parties, and the Arbitration fee shall be borne by the losing parties.

买方:　　　　　　　　　　卖方:
(授权签字)　　　　　　　　(授权签字)

2. Reading: Forward Contracts vs. Futures Contracts

Fundamentally, forward and futures contracts have the same function, with both types of contracts allowing people to buy or sell a specific type of asset at a specific time at a given price. However, it's in the specific details that these contracts differ.

Exchange Traded Versus Private Agreements

First of all, futures contracts are exchange-traded and, therefore, are standardized contracts. Forward contracts, on the other hand, are private agreements between two parties and are not as rigid in their stated terms and conditions. Because forward contracts are private agreements, there is a high counterparty risk —i. e. , a chance that a party may default on its side of the agreement. Futures contracts have clearing houses that guarantee the transactions, which drastically lowers the probability of default to almost never.

Settlement of Contracts

Secondly, the specific details concerning settlement and delivery are quite distinct. For forward contracts, settlement of the contract occurs at the end of the contract. Futures contracts are market-to-market daily, which means that daily changes are settled day by day until the end of the contract. Furthermore, settlement for futures contracts can occur over a range of dates. Forward contracts, on the other hand, only possess one settlement date.

Speculation and Hedging

Lastly, because futures contracts are quite frequently employed by speculators, who bet on the direction in which an asset's price will move, they are usually closed out prior to maturity and delivery usually never happens. On the other hand, forward contracts are mostly used by hedgers that want to eliminate the volatility of an asset's price, and delivery of the asset or cash settlement will usually take place.

 Knowledge Link

☆ 签字仪式的正式程序

签字仪式是签署合同的重要环节，它的时间不长，但程序规范、气氛庄重而热烈。签字仪式的正式程序一共分为四项，它们分别是：

其一，是签字仪式正式开始。有关各方人员进入签字厅，在既定的位次上各就各位。

其二，是签字人正式签署合同文本。通常的做法是，首先签署己方保存的合同文本，再接着签署他方保存的合同文本。

商务礼仪规定：每个签字人在由己方保留的合同文本上签字时，按惯例应当名列首位。因此，每个签字人均应首先签署己方保存的合同文本，然后再交由他方签字人签字。这一做法，在礼仪上称为"轮换制"。它的含义是在位次排列上，轮流使有关各方有机会居于首位一次，以显示机会均等，各方平等。

其三，是签字人正式交换已经有关各方正式签署的合同文本。此时，各方签字人应热烈握手，互致祝贺，并相互交换各自一方刚才使用过的签字笔，以志纪念。全场人员应鼓掌，表示祝贺。

其四，是共饮香槟酒互相道贺。交换已签的合同文本后，有关人员，尤其是签字人当场干上一杯香槟酒，是国际上通行的用以增添喜庆色彩的做法。

在一般情况下，商务合同在正式签署后，应提交有关方面进行公证，此后才正式生效。

Situation 4 Conclusion of Business and the Fulfillment of a Contract

Sum-Up

Some Phrases about Contract

1. To draw up a contract; to draft a contract; to have a contract ready for signature
2. To sign/ close/ enter into a contract
3. To execute/ perform/ fulfill a contract
4. To cancel a contract
5. To violate/ breach/ break a contract

Terms and Conditions

1. The name of the commodity and specification, the quantity and packing
2. Date of shipment and destination port
3. The quoting of prices
4. Terms of payment
5. Insurance
6. Quality and quantity/weight inspection
7. Claim
8. Arbitration
9. Shipping documents required

……

The following Sentences Are Usually Used in Orders and Contracts

1. Orders Received and Confirm

◇ We received your letter of the 10th inst., and thank you for your order for …
 本月 10 日来函收悉，感谢贵方对……的订货。

◇ We are in receipt of your favour of the 10th May, with your order for five printing machines, which I herewith acknowledge with best thanks.
 贵公司 5 月 10 日来函及五部印刷机器的订单均已收到，在此表示感谢。

◇ We confirm herewith your telegraphic order of the 10th June, for 100 cwt. of the best sugar.
 贵公司 6 月 10 日电报关于 100 英担高级砂糖订单已收到，并予以确认。

◇ We acknowledge receipt of your favour of the 10th July, and thank you for the order you have given us.
 贵公司 7 月 10 日函收悉，对此次订货，我公司表示感谢。

2. Cancel or Change Orders

◇ To my deep regret, the buyer of these goods has just cancelled the order, a fact which compels me to cancel my order with you.

非常抱歉,兹因购货人已向我公司撤销订单,迫使我公司只好向贵公司取消这一次订货。

◇ Our requirements are now fully covered for some time to come, and we therefore greatly regret that we have to cancel our order with you.

很抱歉由于我司在今后一段时间内,所有货物品已完全够用,因此不得不取消此次订货,敬请谅解。

◇ We are sorry to report that our buyer does not confirm this order at your price USD 500; we must, therefore, ask you to cancel same.

非常遗憾地通知贵公司,因为购货人对贵公司价格 500 美元不予确认,因此要求您取消此订单。

◇ I regret that I have to notify you of so many orders being cancelled at the same time.

非常遗憾,我公司不得不通知,在此同一时期内,需要取消数种订单。

3. Sending a Contract

◇ We would be grateful if you would sign the contract and return one copy to us for our record as soon as possible.

如贵公司能尽快签署合同并寄回一份供我们备案,我们将不胜感激。

◇ We hope that the contract will be fulfilled smoothly and successfully.

希望本合同能够顺利并成功地履行。

◇ Thank you very much for your cooperation and hope that this may be the beginning of long and friendly relationship between us.

十分感谢贵方的合作,希望此次合作成为我们双方长期友好关系的开端。

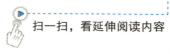 扫一扫,看延伸阅读内容

Situation 05

Terms of Payment

📎 Objectives

1) To be able to translate and write a letter of suggesting a certain term of payment.
2) To be able to translate and write a letter of asking for an easy payment.
3) To be able to translate and write a letter of urging establishment of L/C.
4) To be able to translate and write a letter of asking for amendment to L/C.
5) To be able to translate and write a letter of asking for extension of L/C.

📎 Introduction

Modes of Payment in International Trade

There are three major modes of payment in international trade: remittance, collection and letter of credit (abbreviated to L/C). Remittance and collection are commercial credit offered by companies. The letter of credit is banker's credit offered by banks.

The Main Contents of a Letter on Payment and L/C

Usually, a letter on payment and L/C concerns one of the following topics:
1) Negotiation of the terms of payment happens between the seller and the buyer.
2) The seller urges the buyer to open the L/C.
3) The buyer applies for the establishment of the L/C.
4) The buyer advices the seller of the establishment of the L/C.
5) The seller asks for the amendment of the L/C.
6) The seller asks the buyer to extend the L/C.

Task 1   Suggesting a Certain Term of Payment

Preparing

Relative Reading

Terms of Payment

In foreign trade, buyers and sellers are in two countries. Sometimes, they have to do business with unknown buyers. If the seller delivers goods before payment has been made, he runs certain risks of non-payment of the buyer, and if the buyer makes payment in advance, he likewise runs risks of non-delivery of the goods. It becomes necessary for a third party to act as an intermediate between them to solve the problem of payment. This party is the bank, who either guarantees payment to the seller and examines the seller's shipping documents for the buyer or makes collection for the seller. That is why we say payment in foreign trade is rather complicated.

In recent years, large amounts of overdue debts have occurred in China's foreign trade. Owing to bad management and the disadvantage of enterprise's system, many exporters suffer from failing to recover their foreign exchange. So, every exporter shall pay close attention to terms of payment (支付条款).

Payment terms are the arrangement that you have with your creditor for repaying the obligation to them.

The terms of payment are an important part of the sales contract. From the seller's point of view, the best terms would be full payment in cash at the time of sale, while the buyers would prefer to have the goods before making payment. Importers and exporters are separated from each other by thousands of miles. This adds to the difficulties of coming to an agreement on how payment should be made. The exporters and importers usually meet each other halfway and agree to payment by letter of credit opened by a reliable bank. A letter of credit is a banker's guarantee that payment will be made on presentation of all the required shipment documents. In this way, the sellers or exporters receive a guarantee not only from the buyers or importers, but also from a banker that payment will be made on delivery of the goods. On the other hand, the buyers or importers are given the guarantee that the banker will not make payment unless the shipping documents are presented.

Situation 5　Terms of Payment

Methods of Payment

1. Kinds of payment with times

1）Payment before delivery 交货前付款

2）Payment as delivery 交货时付款

3）Payment after delivery 交货后付款

2. Ways of payment

The first way includes the following：

Transfer / Remittance 汇款

Mail Transfer　　M/T 信汇

Telegraphic Transfer T/T 电汇

Banker's Demand Draft 票汇

The second way includes the following：

Collection 托收

Documents against Payment D/P 付款交单

Documents against Acceptance D/A 承兑交单

The third way includes the following：

Letter of Credit　L/C 信用证

Irrevocable Letter of Credit 不可撤销信用证

Confirmed Letter of Credit 保兑信用证

Divisible Letter of Credit 可分割信用证

Transferable Letter of Credit 可转让信用证

Sight Letter of Credit 即期信用证

Time Letter of Credit 远期信用证

Anticipatory Letter of Credit 预支信用证

Revolving Letter of Credit 循环信用证

Clean Letter of Credit 光票信用证

Documentary Letter of Credit 跟单信用证

✓　**Lead In — Dialogues**

Bob: If it's OK with you, we would like payment prior to delivery, since this is your first order.

Lisa: I understand why you would like it that way, but we prefer payment after delivery, because these goods are very expensive.

Bob: I know they are very expensive, but why does that mean you should pay after delivery?

Lisa: It's a large order, so if we give an advance payment, we will have money trouble, because it will take three or four months to sell the goods and start to make a profit.

Bob: I understand, but if we must pay to make the goods, and then must wait four months for you to pay, we will have money trouble too.

Lisa: Let's do it this way. We will pay in installments, with the first payment to be two weeks after delivery, then once a month after that.

Performing

 Text

Sample 1   Suggesting a Certain Term of Payment

Dear Sirs,

We are pleased to receive your inquiry of 1st August and enclose our illustrated catalogue and price list.

We are confident you will be interested in our products and welcome your further inquiry.

As to our terms of payment, we usually adopt D/A.

Your kindness in giving priority to the consideration of the above request and giving us an early favorable reply would be appreciated.

Yours faithfully,

Sample 2   Reply to the Above

Dear Sirs,

We are in receipt of your letter of August 2nd. Having studied your suggestion for payment by D/A, we regret that we are unable to entertain your request. As our usual practice goes, we require payment by confirmed and irrevocable letter of credit. However, in consideration of our friendly relations, we are prepared to accept D/P as an exceptional case.

We sincerely hope that the above payment term will be acceptable to you and trust you will appreciate our cooperation.

It will be highly appreciated to receive your early reply.

Yours sincerely,

Sample 3   Suggesting a Certain Term of Payment

Dear Sirs,

We received your letter of October 7, 2017 and learn that you are going to sell our

Situation 5　Terms of Payment

products in your country.

We regret that we are unable to consider your request for payment on D/A basis. As a rule, we ask for payment by L/C.

But, in view of our long-term business relations, we will, as an exceptional case, accept payment for your order by D/P at sight. We trust this will greatly facilitate your efforts in sales.

We hope the above payment terms will be acceptable to you and expect to receive your order on good time.

We look forward to your early reply.

Yours faithfully,
Marry

Notes

1) D/P (Documents against Payment)：付款交单，是买方的交单须以进口人的付款为条件，即出口人将汇票连同货运单据交给银行托收时，指示银行只有在进口人付清货款时才能交出货运单据。

   D/A (Documents against Acceptance)：承兑交单，是指在使用远期汇票收款时，当代收行或提示行向进口人提示汇票和单据，若单据合格，进口人对汇票加以承兑，银行即凭进口人的承兑向进口人交付单据。这种托收方式只适用于远期汇票的托收，与付款交单相比，承兑人交单为进口人提供了资金融通上的方便，但出口人的风险增加了。

2) to give priority to the consideration of　优先考虑

3) avorable　利好的，有益的，有利的

4) regret　*vi. vt.* 遗憾，抱歉

   a. regret + *n.*

      e. g. We regret our inability to comply with your wishes.

      我们很抱歉未能依照你方要求办理。

   b. regret + doing

      e. g. We regret being unable to offer you this article at present.

      很抱歉我们现在不能向你方提供这种商品的价格。

   c. regret + to do sth.

      e. g. I regret to say I cannot come.

      很抱歉，我不能来了。

   d. regret + that

      e. g. I regret that I cannot help you.

      我帮不上忙，很抱歉。

e. g. It is to be regretted that …   ……真可惜

5) entertain your request   接受你的请求

   entertain   v. 容纳，接受（请求等）

6) "As our usual practice goes, …"   按照惯例……

7) confirmed letter of credit   保兑信用证

8) in consideration of   考虑到

9) be acceptable to sb.   能够为某人接受

10) highly   非常，十分

   It will be highly appreciated to do sth.   对……十分感激

Practicing

I. Translate the following expressions into English.

优先考虑   利好的，有益的，有利的

……真可惜   接受您的请求

按照惯例   保兑信用证

考虑到   对……十分感激

能够为某人接受   付款交单

II. Choose the best answer to each of the following sentences.

1. Mr. Smith will make a note _____ Mr. Sanchez's request for consular invoice.
   A. of   B. for   C. to   D. against

2. Payments should be made _____ sight draft.
   A. at   B. upon   C. by   D. after

3. Payment by L/C is our method of _____ trade in chemicals.
   A. negotiating   B. settling   C. financing   D. assisting

4. If D/A is possible, it will help ease the _____ problem.
   A. license   B. licensing   C. to license   D. licensed

5. Mr. Yin could agree _____ D/P terms.
   A. with   B. to   C. in   D. over

6. 90% of the credit amount must be paid _____ the presentation of documents.
   A. at   B. by   C. against   D. when

7. Mr. Wood guarantees that Mr. Feng will _____ their equipment.
   A. satisfy   B. satisfactory
   C. be satisfied with   D. satisfy with

8. You don't say whether you wish the transaction to be _____ cash or _____ credit.

A. at　　　　B. by　　　　C. on　　　　D. in

9. We shall be glad if you agree to ship the goods to us as before _____ cash against documents basis.

A. with　　　B. during　　C. in　　　　D. on

10. We have opened an L/C in your favor _____ the amount of RMB 20,000.

A. on　　　　B. in　　　　C. by　　　　D. at

III. Translate the following sentences into Chinese.

1. With regard to terms of payment, we regret being unable to accept payment by documents against payment.

2. Among the clauses specified in your Credit No. 0009, we regret to find the following two do not conform to the contract stipulations.

3. The 900 Children scooters under S/C No. 998 have been packed, but we have not yet received the covering L/C.

4. Our bank's correspondent, Bank of China, Ningbo, will soon advise you of the credit, and you are authorized to draw on them at 45 days for the amount of the invoice value.

5. You may draw on our bank at sight for the full amount of the invoice, and your draft should be presented together with the following documents.

IV. Translate the following sentences into English.

1. 按你方要求，我们破例接受即期付款交单，但只此一次，下不为例。

2. 我们建议以见票30天付款的汇票，承税交单，你方若接受，请确认。

3. 货已备妥待装，请即来电告知确切开证日期。

4. 请速开信用证，以便赶装预定于五月底到达你港的直达船。

5. 若有关信用证能在三月十五号开到，可保证准时装运。

V. Write a letter about suggesting a certain term of payment (open).

Supplement

Supplementary Reading

1. Letter

Dear Ms Li

Order No. 8752

Thank you for your order which is being sent to you today.

As agreed we have forwarded our bill, No. 120 for USD 1,830 with the documents to your bank, Industrial & Commercial Bank of China, Caohejing Branch, Shanghai. The Draft has been made out for payment 30 days after sight, and the documents will be handed to you on acceptance.

Yours sincerely,

H. Kotler

Managing Director

2. Reading: Cash Is One of Ways to Pay for Your Purchases

Cash (Bills and Change). There are a variety of ways to pay for your purchases, and cash is one of the most common and familiar. Both paper money (of varying denominations) and coins are included under the larger category of "cash". While cash has the advantage of being immediate, it is not the most secure form of payment. If it is lost or destroyed, that money is essentially gone. There is no recourse to recoup those losses. If you have a torn bill and are unsure whether it is still usable, check with your nearest bank. Cash is used exclusively at physical retailers. There is no way to use cash towards your online purchases.

Debit Card. A debit card is an increasingly popular way to pay for both online and retailer purchases. It looks exactly like a credit card, but it functions in a different manner. Unlike a credit card, paying with a debit card takes the money directly out of your checking account. In this way, it is almost exactly like writing a personal check, but without all the hassle of filling out that check. For more information about how to use this form of payment.

Debit cards can be acquired from your bank. You can request one in person or request one at your bank's website.

Credit Card. A credit card is one of the most popular ways to make purchases which are more expensive than your everyday buys, although they can be used on purchases of any amount.

Credit cards look almost exactly like debit cards, and using them is sometimes referred to as paying with "plastic." Rather than paying for the item right away, paying with a credit card temporarily defers your bill. At the end of each month, you will receive a credit card statement with an itemized list of all your purchases. Therefore, rather than paying the retailer directly, you pay off your bill to the credit card company. If you don't pay the entire balance of the bill, the company is authorized to charge you interest on your remaining balance. Credit cards can be used for both online purchases and at physical retailers.

Gift Certificate. A gift certificate is a less common form of payment, but they are increasingly becoming a popular gift. Thus, they are increasingly becoming a popular form of payment. Gift certificates come in several forms, but they are essentially prepaid certificates with a certain amount of money added to that certificate. They can be purchased for one particular store, several stores, or any participating store. They come in plastic card form, paper form, or electronic form.

Depending on the type of gift certificate, they can be redeemed（兑现；偿还）at physical retailers（实体零售商）, online retailers, or both.

✔ **Knowledge Link**

☆ 国际结算的方式

1. 汇付

汇付（Remittance）是指一国的进口商或其他付款人委托出口商或其他收款人所在国的第三方（一般为银行），对收款人支付一定金额，而不靠输送现金来结算彼此间债权债务关系的一种支付方式。一般在预付货款、支付佣金、支付样品费、代垫费用、履约保证金及赔款等方面用得较多。最通常的汇款方式有：电汇、信汇与票汇三种。

2. 托收

托收是指一国出口商主动向另一国进口商索款时，开具以进口商为付款人的汇票，委托第三方（银行）向进口方代收货款。托收分为光票托收和跟单托收两种。

1）光票托收（Clean Collection）是指出口人（出票人）开具汇票，不附随任何货运单据托收。这种子方式通常用于收取货款尾数和样品费、佣金、代垫费用等贸易从属费用。

2）跟单托收（Collection）根据交单条件不同分为付款交单（D/P，按付款时间又分为即期付款交单和远期付款交单）和承兑交单（D/A，只有远期承兑交单）。承兑交单支付方式对出口收汇风险很大，使用时要十分慎重。

3. 信用证

信用证（Letter of Credit）是银行根据进口人的请求开给出口人的一种保证支付货款的书面凭证。在信用证内开证行授权出口人在符合信用证规定的条款和条件下，以该行或其他指定银行为付款人，开具不得超过信用证规定金额的汇票，并随附信用证的各种单据，按信用证规定的议付时间和指定地点收取货款。

Task 2 Asking for an Easy Payment

Preparing

Relative Reading

1. Advantages & Disadvantages of a Letter of Credit

Advantages to the Exporter

Shifts credit risk from the importer to the importer's bank (issuing bank).

An undertaking from the issuing bank that payment will be made under the letter of credit, provided that you meet all terms and conditions of the letter of credit.

If the letter of credit is not issued as agreed, you are not obligated to ship against it.

Disadvantages to the Exporter

Documents must be prepared in strict compliance with the requirements stipulated in the letter of credit. Non-compliance leaves you exposed to risk of non-payment and removes the protection afforded by the issuing bank since the final decision on the documents then rests with the importer.

2. Risks in Documentary Collections

For the Exporter

If it is a sight draft, the exporter will reduce the risk of non-payment but will not eliminate it totally since the importer may not be in a position to pay for the goods or may not be able to procure sufficient foreign exchange to make the payment. In this case the exporter may be forced to either call back the goods or negotiate sale to some other interested party, which may be at a reduced rate.

In the case of term draft, the risk to the exporter is higher since the foreign buyer will take possession of the goods and may not pay at due date, forcing therefore the exporter to try and collect payment from the foreign buyer in the foreign buyer's home country.

For the Importer

The importer faces the risk of paying for goods of sub-standard quality or even with shortages. In such a circumstance, it would take some time to get refunds from the exporter. It could also happen that the exporter refuses to make refunds, leading the importer to lengthy legal proceedings.

3. Advantages and Disadvantages of Documentary Collection

The major advantage of a "cash against documents" payment method for the buyer is the low cost, versus opening a letter of credit. The advantage for the seller is that he can receive full payment prior to releasing control of the documents, although this is offset by the risk that the buyer will, for some reason, reject the documents (or they will not be in order). Since the cargo would already be loaded (to generate the documents), the seller has little recourse against the buyer in case of non-payment. A payment against documents arrangement involves a high level of trust between the seller and the buyer and should be adopted only by parties well known to each other.

4. Payment Instruments of International Trade

In international trade, payment can be made by various means: drafts, promissory notes, checks, money orders, credit cards (汇票；本票；支票；汇票；信用卡).

5. Draft/ Bill of Exchange

It is an unconditional order in writing signed by one party (drawer) requesting a second party (drawee/payer) to make payment in lawful money immediately or at a determinable future time to a third party (payee).

✔ Lead In — Dialogues

Lisa: We are having a little trouble selling the goods, so we want to ask if we could defer payment until the end of the month.

Bob: I can't accept that, because this will be the second time you have not met the agreed-upon payment schedule. I will get in trouble if I let you defer again.

Lisa: OK. Would it be alright if we make the initial payment in two weeks, then pay in one-month installments after that?

Bob: I'll have to check with my manager, but I think it will be alright if you promise there will be no more delays after that.

Lisa: I give you my word that payments will be made on time from now on. And I will make the initial payment a lump sum payment of half the total.

Bob: That is even better. I'll phone you tomorrow to let you know what my manager says.

Performing

Text

Sample 1 Asking for an Easy Payment

Dear Sirs,

In the past, our purchases of children's jackets No. 102 from you have normally been paid by confirmed, irrevocable letter of credit.

This arrangement has cost us a great deal of money. From the moment we open the credit until our buyers pay us normally ties up funds for about three months. This is currently a particularly serious problem for us in view of the difficult economic climate and the prevailing high interest rates.

If you could offer us easier payment terms, it would probably lead to an increase in business between our companies. We propose either cash against documents on arrival of goods, or drawing on us at three months' sight.

We hope our request will meet with your agreement and look forward to your early reply.

Yours faithfully,
Tony Blare

Sample 2 Asking for an Easy Payment

Dear Sirs,

We would like to place an order for 500 children's jackets at your price of USD 300 each, CIF Lagos, for shipment during July/August.

We would like to pay for this order by a 60-day L/C. This is a big order involving USD 150,000 and, since we have only moderate cash reserves, tying up funds for three or four months would cause problems for us.

We much appreciate the support you have given us in the past and would be most grateful if you could extend this favour to us. If you are agreeable, please send us your contract. On receipt, we will establish the relevant L/C immediately.

Yours faithfully,
Tony Blare

Situation 5　Terms of Payment

Sample 3　Asking for an Easy Payment.

Dear Qinyu,

Thank you for your letter of 4th April, which arrived this morning.

We are pleased that you have been able to ship our order in good time but we are surprised that you still demand D/P. After long years of satisfactory trading we feel that we are entitled to（有……的资格；有权）easier terms. Most of our suppliers are drawing on us at D/A 60 days after sight and we should be grateful if you could grant us the same terms.

We are looking forward to your favorable reply.

Yours faithfully,

Notes

1) cost　*vt.* 要价；价值（若干）；费；需

　　e. g. How much did that bag cost?

　　　　那个书包多少钱？

2) tie up　占用，管制，冻结（金钱、财物）

3) in view of　鉴于；由于；为了

　　view　*n.* 视野；见解 *v.* 考虑；看

　　a field of view　视野

　　a point of view　观点

4) prevailing　*adj.* 占优势的，主要的，流行的

5) propose　*v.* 计划，建议，向……提议

　　e. g. I propose to go on Tuesday.

　　　　我想星期二去。

6) place an order　下订单

　　e. g. We would like to place an order with you for the Article No. 102.

　　　　我方想向贵方订购102号产品。

7) moderate　*adj.* 中等的，适度的，适中的

　　a moderate price　适度的价格

　　a moderate climate　温和的气候

8) be most grateful if...　如能……将不胜感激

9) extend this favour　提供帮助

10) establish the relevant L/C　开立相关信用证

Practicing

I. Translate the following expressions into English.

要价；价值　　　　　　　占用

鉴于；由于　　　　　　　占优势的，主要的，流行的

计划，建议　　　　　　　下订单

提供帮助　　　　　　　　开立相关信用证

如能……将不胜感激　　　适度的价格

II. Translate the following expressions into Chinese.

1. payment by cash ‖ cash payment ‖ payment by ready cash
2. payment by bill
3. payment in full ‖ full payment
4. payment on term
5. annual payment
6. monthly payment ‖ monthly installment
7. deferred payment
8. prompt payment ‖ immediate payment
9. cash on deliver (C. O. D.)
10. cash on arrival

III. Translate the following sentences into Chinese.

1. Please protect our draft on presentation.
2. We've drawn on you for payment of the invoice amounting to USD 20,000.
3. We'll agree to change the terms of payment from L/C at sight to D/P at sight.
4. Your draft will be honoured on presentation.
5. We'll draw on you by our documentary draft at sight on collection basis.

IV. Translate the following sentences into English.

1. 用英镑付款较方便。
2. 您希望用什么方式付款？
3. 我们可以按60天付款交单的方式进行交易。
4. 我们不能接受延期付款。
5. 这是国际贸易中惯用的付款方式。

V. Write a letter about asking for an easy payment (open).

Situation 5   Terms of Payment

Supplement

✓ Supplementary Reading

1. Letter

Dear Sirs,

Thank you for your order for 600 Irina 262 typewriters by your letter of 18 May.

We have considered your proposal to pay by a 20-day letter of credit. We do not usually accept time credit. However, in view of our long and mutually beneficial relationship, we are willing to make an exception this time.

I must stress that this departure from our usual practice relates to this transaction only. We cannot regard it as setting a precedent for future transactions.

I enclose our sales contract No. 86 covering the order. I would be grateful if you would follow the usual procedure.

Yours faithfully,

Liyun

2. The Mode of Payment

It includes remittance (T/T, M/T, D/D), collection (D/P, D/A) and L/C. L/C is the most frequently adopted mode of payment in China's foreign trade.

3. Remittance

In international trade, this is the simplest way to transfer funds.

It means the transfer of money from one party to another party through banks of different countries, that is, a bank (the remitting bank) at the request of its customer (the remitter), transfers a certain sum of money to its overseas branch.

4. Documentary Collection

Collection is the process wherein a bank, in accordance with the seller's instruction, handles documents in order to deliver to the buyer against payment, acceptance, or on other terms and conditions.

Banks act as intermediaries, protecting the interests of both parties.

5. Types of Documentary Collection

There are two types of documentary collection: documents against payment (D/P) and documents against acceptance (D/A).

D/P can be further subdivided into D/P at sight and D/P after sight.

In such cases, banks are only responsible to collect or remit the payment and will not be liable for non-payment.

6. Documents against Acceptance (D/A)

Documents against acceptance means that the title documents will be released to the buyer after the buyer's acceptance of the usance draft drawn on him. Payment will be made when the usance period is due. Under this term, as the importer gets the goods before making payment, the importer's credit standing is important to the exporter. It is therefore not as secure as D/P since the seller might not be paid at all.

7. Advantages of Using Documentary

Using documentary collection has a number of advantages to sellers.

1) Sellers or banks control shipping documents that represent title to the goods until buyers pay or accept the draft.

2) Payment under collection is more immediate and less expensive.

3) Compared with L/C, collection has less complicated procedures.

8. Disadvantages of Using Documentary Collection

1) Collection time may be longer than letters of credit and cash in advance. And document inspection is not done by banks, which only act as the agent to present documents.

2) Payment is not guaranteed by the bank as an L/C arrangement. Collection relies on a buyer's credit instead of that of a bank's. Sellers will face the risks of insolvency in case of bankruptcy or breach of contract of buyers or other political and economical affairs of the importing countries.

3) Under D/A, release of documents occurs prior to payment, and sellers will lose control on both goods and funds.

✓ Knowledge Link

☆ 出口较安全的收款方式

出口最根本的目的就是为了回收货款。任何一笔交易都应该建立在平等互利的基础上。

1. 30% T/T 定金 + 70% 即期、保兑、不可撤销的信用证。

2. 100% 即期、保兑、不可撤销的信用证 + CIF 的运输条款。

3. 即期、保兑、不可撤销的信用证 + FOB。(最好自己来安排到达目的港的船公司,并与船公司有良好合作关系,以求掌控货物)

4. 30% T/T 定金 + 70% 见提单传真件付款。(此付款方式适用于贸易额较小的业务。如果贸易额度较大，不应采用此付款方式。因为我们无法保证外商对货物的最终需求。外商可能因市场的变化而放弃交易。）

其他付款方式（国际贸易书本上提及的付款方式）不要轻易采用。

☆ 出口较安全的收款国家与地区

1. 美国：美国的商业信誉管理系统较完善。
2. 欧洲国家：主要指英国、法国、德国、西班牙、比利时、荷兰等。
3. 加拿大、澳大利亚、日本、韩国及中国香港。

Task 3 Urging Establishment of L/C

Preparing

Relative Reading

Principles of Writing Letters Urging Establishment of L/C

No suggestion of annoyance is allowed to be shown in the letter urging establishment of L/C. It is not advisable, except under special conditions, to start off too strongly by blaming the buyer for not executing the contract. The first message sent should therefore be a polite note saying that the goods ordered are ready but the relevant letter of credit has not yet be received. If the first message brings no reply, a second one will be sent. This one, though still restrained, will express disappointment and surprise.

The Following Structure is for Your Reference in Writing a Letter Urging Establishment of L/C

1) Open the letter in a positive way. For example, in the first paragraph the seller usually informs the buyer that the goods are ready for dispatch or that the shipping space has already been booked.

2) Politely push the buyers to open the L/C without delay, either by referring to the stipulations of the contract or by reminding the buyers of the seriousness of not opening the L/C in time.

3) Express expectations and ask the buyers to take immediate action.

Writing Step for Urging Establishment of L/C

Inform that the goods contracted has been ready for shipping.

Remind that the covering L/C has not been received.

Request for expediting establishment L/C.

Hope to receive early response.

The Response of Urging Establishment of L/C

Refer to the previous letter.

Inform that the covering L/C has been opened and sent.

Hope that the shipping advice can be received early.

Writing Tips

When urging the buyer to establish the relative L/C, the seller should draft the letter or E-mail skillfully by using proper language to show your determination but not to harm the relationship between two parties.

Usually a letter or E-mail focusing on urging the buyer to establish the relative L/C by the seller often consists of the following parts:

1) Mention the contract No., order No. of the goods in the opening sentences.

2) State the reasons why you need to inform or urge the buyer to open the L/C.

3) Urge the buyer to open the L/C ASAP.

✓ Lead in — Dialogues

Bob: Hello, could I speak to Lisa, please?

Lisa: Morning! Lisa speaking. What can I do for you?

Bob: Hi, Lisa. This is Bob from ABC company. I would like to ask about the L/C No. 101. We've not got any news about it.

Lisa: Oh Bob, no worries. Our letter of credit will be opened early March.

Bob: Please open the L/C 20 to 30 days before the date of delivery.

Lisa: No problem, I assure you that we will do it strictly as the contract stipulated.

Performing

✓ Text

Sample 1   Asking for Establishment of L/C

Gentlemen,

Thank you for your order No. 105. In order to execute it, please open an irrevocable L/C for the amount of USD 80,000 in our favor. This account shall be available until Oct. 20.

Upon arrival of the L/C we will pack and ship the order as requested.

Sincerely,

Sample 2 A Reply to theLetter of Asking for Establishment of L/C

Dear Sirs,

Thank you for your letter of June 18 enclosing details of your terms. According to your request for opening an irrevocable L/C, we have instructed the Beijing City Commercial Bank to open a credit for USD 80,000 in your favor, valid until Oct. 20. Please advise us by fax when the order has been executed.

Sincerely,

Sample 3 Urging Establishment of L/C

Dear Sirs,

Re: Your Order No. 106 for cotton T-shirts.

With reference to our faxes dated the 20th of Sept. requesting you to establish the L/C covering the above mentioned order we regret having received no news from you up till now.

We wish to remind you that it was agreed that you would establish the required L/C upon receipt of our confirmation when placing the order. Now we are placed in a very embarrassing situation now that one month has elapsed and nothing whatsoever has been heard from you. As the goods have been ready for shipment for quite some time, you are supposed to take immediate action, particularly since we can't think of any valid reason for further delaying the opening of the credit.

Yours truly,

Sample 4 A Reply to the Letter Asking for Establishment of L/C

Dear Sirs,

Re: Our Order No. 106 for cotton T-shirts.

We have received your faxes dated 20th of Sept. urging us to establish the L/C for the captioned order.

We are very sorry for the delay in opening the L/C, which was due to an oversight of our staff. However, when found it, we immediately opened the covering credit with the Bank of China, and trust the same will reach you soon.

Please allow us to express again our regret for the inconvenience that has been caused to you.

Yours faithfully,

Notes

1) execute *vt.* 执行，实行，完成

   e. g. He asked his nephew to execute his will.
   他请自己的侄子执行遗嘱。

2) "…open an irrevocable L/C for the amount of USD 80,000 in our favor."
   请开立以我方为受益人的金额为 80,000 美元的不可撤销信用证。
   to open an irrevocable L/C for the amount of …in one's favor
   开立以某人为受益人的金额为……的不可撤销信用证

3) term *n.* 条款，条件
   to come to terms with   与……达成协议

4) instruct *v.* 命令，指示
   to instruct sb. to do sth.   指示某人做某事

5) advise *v.* 通知；告知
   e. g. We are to advise you that the matter is under consideration.
   此事已在讨论中，特此通知。

6) date *v.* 注明日期；记日期
   e. g. Don't forget to date your letters. 别忘了在你的信上写明日期。

7) up till now   到现在为止

8) are supposed to   被期望或要求；应该

9) valid reason for sth.   ……的正当理由

10) urge *v.* 催促；怂恿
    e. g. He urged her to rest. 他催促她休息。

11) captioned order   上述订单

12) due to   由于

13) oversight *n.* 勘漏，失察，疏忽
    e. g. Even an oversight in the design might issue in heavy losses.
    设计中哪怕是一点点疏忽也可能造成重大的损失。

Practicing

I. Translate the following expressions into English.

执行，实行   开立以某人为收益人的金额为……的不可撤销信用证
指示某人做某事   通知；告知
到现在为止   由于
被期望或要求；应该   勘漏，失察，疏忽
……的正当理由   上述订单

Situation 5　Terms of Payment

II. Choose the best answer to the each of the following sentences.
1. Payments should be made _____ sight draft.
   A. at　　　　　B. upon　　　　C. by　　　　　D. after
2. We have arranged with our bank for an L/C to be _____ .
   A. opened　　　B. issued　　　C. established　　D. A/ B /C
3. We have made _____ that we would not accept payment by D/A for your present order.
   A. clear　　　　B. that clear　　C. this clear　　　D. it clear
4. 90% of the credit amount must be paid _____ presentation of documents.
   A. at　　　　　B. by　　　　　C. against　　　　D. for
5. We believe the above terms of payment will prove _____ .
   A. satisfy　　　B. satisfactory　C. satisfied　　　D. satisfaction
6. We have opened an L/C in your favour _____ the amount of RMB 20, 000.
   A. on　　　　　B. in　　　　　C. by　　　　　D. at
7. If the amount exceeds that figure, payment _____ L/C will be required.
   A. at　　　　　B. by　　　　　C. for　　　　　D. in
8. It is our usual practice to _____ you at sight as soon as shipment is made.
   A. advise　　　B. notify　　　C. pay　　　　　D. draw on
9. The goods _____ if your L/C had arrived by the end of November last.
   A. would be shipped already　　　B. must have shipped already
   C. had been shipped already　　　D. would have been shipped already
10. We shall be glad if you will _____ the matter at once and let us know the reason for the delay in opening the L/C.
    A. look into　　B. look for　　C. look after　　D. Look on

III. Translate the following sentences into Chinese.
　　1. We have today instructed our bank, the Frank Bank in London to open a confirmed, irrevocable letter of credit in your favor with partial shipment and transshipment allowed clause, available by draft at sight, against surrendering the full set of shipping documents to the negotiating bank.
　　2. In view of the small amount of this transaction, we are prepared to accept payment by D/P at sight (or 30 days' sight) for the value of the goods shipped.
　　3. We wish to draw your attention to the fact that as a special sign of encouragement, we shall consider accepting payment by D/P during this sales-pushing stage. We trust this will greatly facilitate your efforts in sales, and we await your favorable reply.
　　4. You should notice this from the very beginning that we only accept our normal way of

payment, that is, letter of credit at sight. We hope you will respect our rules.

5. Payment is to be made against sight draft drawn under a confirmed, irrevocable, divisible and transferable letter of credit without recourse for the full amount of purchase.

IV. Translate the following into Chinese or English.

1. Translate the following letter into Chinese.

Dear Sirs,

Thank you very much for your letter of the first May, 2018 informing us of the establishment of your L/C No. H-1022 against our S/C No. ZF110103. The L/C in question has just come to hand. However, upon checking, we regret to have found that there are certain clauses which do not conform to those of the contract. Hereby we list the following discrepancies for your attention.

1) The amount of the credit should be USD 152,000 (Say US Dollars one hundred and fifty-two thousand only) instead of USD 125,000.

2) The B/L should be marked "freight prepaid" instead of "freight to collect".

3) The credit should expire on July 15, 2018 for negotiation in China instead of June 30, 2018.

We hope you will make the necessary amendments as early as possible so as to facilitate our shipping arrangement.

Your prompt attention to the above will be highly appreciated.

Yours faithfully,

2. Translate the following sentences into English.

1) 货已备妥待装，请即来电告知确切开证日期。一旦收到该证，即予装运。

2) 请速开信用证，以便赶装预定于五月底到达你港的直达船。

3) 若有关信用证能在三月十五日开到，可保证准时装运。

4) 如果贵方不按期开证，因延迟开证而引起的损失，概由贵方负责。

5) 货已久存码头仓库待运，我方不能无限期等待有关信用证。请速开证。

V. Fill in the blanks with a proper word.

1. The seller should, if necessary, require the buyer to make an amendment _____ the L/C _____ shipment.

2. _____ reference _____ 8,000 pairs of Sheepskin Slippers _____ the sales confirmation No. 578, we have not received your _____ L/C _____ to date.

3. We would like to _____ your attention _____ the _____ that the shipment date is _____, we must point out that unless your L/C _____ us by the end of this month, we shall not be able to _____ shipment _____ the contracted time.

4. We apologize _____ you _____ not having established the relative L/C in time.

5. We wish to call your attention to the validity _____ the L/C, since there is no possibility _____ L/C extension.

6. We would like to make it _____ that the covering L/C should be established _____ time, otherwise it will put us _____ great trouble.

7. _____ compliance _____ the terms _____ payments _____ in the contract, please open a confirmed and irrevocable L/C _____ our favor.

8. The expiry date of your L/C falls _____ May 15, which won't leave us enough time _____ negotiation _____ the document.

VI. Writing practice.

1. Write a letter about urging establishment of L/C.
2. Write a letter of confirming L/C application according to the above.

Supplement

Supplementary Reading

1. Letter

Dear Sirs,

Our Sales Confirmation No. TE162

Reference is made to the 1,000 cartons of Canned Asparagus (罐装芦笋) under the subjected sales confirmation, we wish to draw your attention to the fact that the date of delivery is approaching, but up to the present we have not received the covering Letter of Credit. Please do your utmost to expedite its establishment, so that we may execute the order within the prescribed time.

In order to avoid subsequent amendments, please see to it that the L/C stipulations are in exact accordance with the terms of the contract.

We look forward to receiving your favorable response at an early date.

Yours faithfully,

2. Reading: Urging Establishment of L/C

The Connotation of Urging Establishment of L/C

It is the usual practice in our export trade that the L/C is to be established and to reach the seller one month prior to the date of shipment so as to give the seller ample time to make preparations for shipment, such as making the goods ready and booking shipping space.

However, there may be circumstances where the buyer fails to establish the L/C, or the

L/C does not reach the seller in time.

Then, a letter, usually a telex or fax has to be sent to the buyer to urge him to expedite the L/C or to ascertain its whereabouts.

Whatever the cause may be, it is always annoying to the seller, but it's still not good to appear your annoyance in your urging letter.

Otherwise they will give offence to the buyer and bring about unhappy consequences.

Messages Urging Establishment of L/C Must be Written with Tact

1. Try to be polite to tell the buyer that the goods ordered are ready.
2. Maybe could ask the reason why the L/C still not be issued.
3. Persuade the buyer to fulfill his obligations and open the L/C as soon as possible.

✔ Knowledge Link

☆ 开立信用证通常采用的几种方法

1）信开信用证：开证行根据开证申请人的要求，将信用证的全部内容用信函方式开出，邮寄到通知行，再通知受益人。开证行与通知行之间应事先建立代理行关系，互换签字样本和密押，以便通知行可凭签字样本核对信开信用证上开证行的签字。这种开证方式时间长，但费用较低。对于装运日期较长或金额较小的信用证通常以信开方式开出。

2）简电开证：开证行根据开证申请人的要求，将信用证的主要内容发电预先通知受益人。这种简电信用证只供受益人备货订仓参考，不能凭以装运货物，它也不是有效的信用证文件，银行不能凭以付款/承兑/议付。发出简电通知的开证行必须毫不延迟地向通知行寄送有效信用证文件，受益人方可凭以议付单据。

3）全电开证：开证行根据开证申请人的要求，将信用证的全部内容以加注密押的电讯方式通知受益人所在地的银行，请其通知受益人。目前，外汇指定银行大多用 SWIFT 电讯方式开证。

Task 4　Asking for Amendment to L/C

📝 Preparing

✔ Relative Reading

When Asking for Amendment to an L/C, it is Essential to

1) In the opening sentences thank the customer for the L/C you received and give a

detailed description about it.

2) Give the reasons why you have to ask for the amendment to the L/C.

3) Tender apologies, should we be the responsible party? If not, omit this step.

4) Express your appreciation for the amendment and state your good will to make prompt shipment.

The Letter of Amendment of L/C Usually Includes

1) Refer to the number of L/C.

   Thank you for your L/C…

   We have received your L/C…

2) State the discrepancies in the L/C.

   It appears that the amount in your L/C is insufficient.

3) Request for amending L/C and will effect shipment on receipt of the amendment.

✔ Lead In — Dialogues

Bob: Lisa, we have received your L/C. Thank you for it.

Lisa: Oh, that's great!

Bob: But when we studied it, we found some discrepancies.

Lisa: Really? Please tell me in details.

Bob: Okay. First, the beneficiary of the L/C should be China National Corporation, Beijing instead of Nanjing.

Lisa: Ok, that should be spelling mistakes. Sorry, Bob.

Bob: Second, according to the contract stipulation, the amount should be USD 1,000, but the credit is short opened to the amount of USD 100.

Lisa: Terribly sorry for that. I will make the amendments immediately. And I'm sure such kind of mistakes will not occur again.

Performing

✔ Text

Sample 1   Asking for Amendment to L/C

Dear Mr. Mike,

We are glad to receive your L/C No. B107 established against the S/C No. MH-FS001, but much to our regret, there are some discrepancies between the L/C and the S/C. Hereby we list them below for your attention:

1) The correct name of beneficiary is "NNC IMP. & EXP. CORP."
2) The transshipment term is "allowed" not "prohibited".
3) The port of loading should be "Shanghai" instead of "Ningbo".
4) The freight on B/L should be "collect" not "prepaid".

Thank you for your kind cooperation. Please see to it that L/C amendment reach us not later than Oct. 1, 2011. Failing which we shall not be able to effect shipment in time.

We anticipate your early reply.

Yours faithfully,

Sample 2 Asking for Amendment to L/C

Dear Sirs,

Letter of Credit No. 3526 issued by the Bank of New South Wales has duly arrived. On perusal, we find that transshipment and partial shipment are not allowed.

As direct steamers to your port are few and far between, we have to ship via Hong Kong more often than not. As to partial shipment, it would be to our mutual benefit if we could ship immediately whatever is ready instead of waiting for the whole shipment to be completed. Therefore, we are asking you to amend your L/C to read part shipments and transshipment allowed.

We shall appreciate it if you will modify promptly the L/C as requested.

Yours faithfully,

Sample 3 Asking for Amendment to L/C

Dear Sirs,

Thank you for your irrevocable L/C opened through Bank of China for 10 cases of bottled medicine.

According to the stipulations of the L/C, the total quantity should be shipped not later than February 10. Although we have been making great efforts to book shipping on time, much to our regret, we were told by the shipping companies contracted that there would be no shipping container before January 24. Therefore, we hereby request you to have both the date of shipment and validity of the L/C extended not later than February 15 and 30 respectively.

Since this is an urgent matter, please amend the L/C immediately. Your compliance with our request will be highly appreciated.

Yours truly,

Notes

1) discrepancy 差异，偏差，误差
2) for your attention 以引起贵方注意

for your reference 供您参考

for your file 供您存档

3) instead of 代替，而不是

4) see to 负责，注意

5) not later than 不迟于

6) effect shipment 实施装运

7) perusal n. 熟读，精读

8) effect shipment 实施装运

9) more often than not 时常

10) to our mutual benefit 对你我双方都有利，符合双方利益

Practicing

I. Translate the following expressions into English.

差异，偏差，误差　　　　　以引起贵方注意

代替，而不是　　　　　　　负责，注意

不迟于　　　　　　　　　　供您存档

实施装运　　　　　　　　　时常

符合双方利益　　　　　　　装船日期

II. Translate the following sentences into Chinese.

1. We find that the following two points do not conform to the contract.

2. Please delete "transshipment not allowed" as direct steamers to your port are not available and transshipment at Hong Kong is necessary.

3. Your prompt attention to the matter will be much appreciated.

4. We will not be able to ship the goods in time if the amendments to the L/C come too late.

5. We have instructed our bank to make an amendment to the L/C No. 378 as requested.

III. Write a letter in English asking for amendment to the following letter of credit by checking it with given contract terms.

XYZ Bank

March 16, 2016

Irrevocable Credit No. 78910

Shanghai Textiles Corporation,

　　You are hereby authorized to draw on at sight to the extent of USD 15,000 (Say US Dollars Fifteen Thousand Only) for account of New York Company. Your drafts to be accompanied by

> Commercial invoice in duplicate
>
> Customs invoice
>
> Full set of clean on board bills of lading made out to order and blank endorsed, marked "freight prepaid" dated not later than May 31, 2006.
>
> Evidencing shipments of 300 bolts of gray cloth CFR New York, from China port to New York, details as per your S/C No. 06/345.
>
> Partial shipments are not allowed. Transshipment is allowed.
>
> This credit expires on May 15, 2006 in China.
>
> 第 06/345 号合同主要条款：
>
> 买方：纽约贸易公司
>
> 卖方：上海纺织公司
>
> 　　灰布　300，每匹 52 美元 CFR 纽约
>
> 　　2006 年 5 月由中国运往纽约，如有必要可以转船或分批装运，不可撤销即期信用证付款，议付有效期为最后装船期后 15 天在中国到期。

Ⅳ. Write a letter about amendment of L/C（open）.

Supplement

✔ Supplementary Reading

1. Letter 1

Dear Sirs,

Re: Your L/C No. 5454

We have received your captioned L/C. Among the clauses specified in your credit we find that the following two points do not conform to the relative contract:

a. Your credit calls for Manufacturer's Certificates, which is not included in the contract. In fact, the contracted commodity is a kind of agricultural produce. It is impossible to obtain a manufacturer's certificate.

b. The contract number is 98/1245 instead of 97/1245. As the goods are now ready for shipment, you are requested amend your credit as soon as possible.

Yours faithfully,

2. Letter 2

Dear Sirs,

Re: L/C No. 336 issued by Citibank (花旗银行)

We have received the above L/C established by you in payment for your order No. 678 covering 300 cases of …

When we checked the L/C with the relevant contract, we found that the amount in your L/C is insufficient. The correct total CIF New York value of your order comes to USD 3,750 instead of USD 3,550, the difference being USD 300.

Your L/C allows us only half a month to effect delivery. But when we signed the contract we have agreed that the delivery should be made within one month upon receipt of the L/C.

As to packing, the contract stipulates that the goods should be packed in cartons and reinforced with nylon straps outside, but your L/C required metal straps instead. We think we should arrange the packing according to the contract.

In view of the above, you are kindly requested to increase the amount of your L/C by USD 300, extend the shipment and validity to September 15 and 30 respectively, as well as amend the term of packing. Meanwhile please advise us by fax.

Yours faithfully,

3. Amendment of L/C

1) Upon receipt of the L/C, the seller should examine it thorough to see whether the clauses in the L/C are in full conformity with the terms stated in the S/C.

2) The discrepancies can cause the negotiating bank dishonoring the payment.

3) After finding the discrepancies, the seller should send an advice to the buyer, asking him to make amendment.

4. Why Sometimes We Should Amend the L/C?

If the exporter finds the clauses (条款) or terms of L/C are not in accordance with the contract and are not convenient for him to collect safely, he should contact the importer and revise the L/C through the issuing bank.

After all, if the exporter and importer could not reach an agreement, they would cancel the L/C or choose another payment terms.

5. Some Reasons For L/C Amendment

To extend the validity time of the L/C.

To extend the validity time for the shipment.

To amend the amount of money.

To amend the specification and the name of the commodity.

To amend the name of the shipping vessel.

To amend the bill of lading.

To amend the mode of loading.

To amend the place for load and unload.

To amend some clauses in the L/C.

To amend the L/C itself, such as a revocable L/C to an irrevocable L/C.

6. What Should We do About Amendment?

We should write a letter to ask for amendment of L/C which includes the following 3 points:

Beginning: express gratitude to the other side for the opening L/C and cite the number.

The main content of amendment: specify the clauses and terms you are not content with and ask him to make a change as you wish.

Ending: thank the other side for cooperation and look forward to receiving the amendment of an L/C.

7. Letters of L/C Amendment

1) Reference: L/C No, Contract No., Order No., name of commodity.

2) What's wrong with the said L/C.

3) Why is it wrong? (against the contract, against our usual practice).

4) Ask for the correct amendment (give out the correct amendment).

5) No amendment, no shipment.

6) Positive ending (prompt amendment).

Knowledge Link

☆ 为什么单据会有不符点？

首先，不符点产生的最直接也是最常见的原因是公司制单员的业务知识局限和操作疏忽。

因为业务范围的限制，一家公司可能与欧洲公司的业务较多，与中东及其他国家的业务量不大，或者情况正好相反，而每个地区的信用证又有不同特点，如欧洲的信用证较为规范，中东来证大多条款较为复杂，要求的单据多，有些单据要求还较为独特——这就决定了业务员不可能对所有类型的信用证均熟悉。

其次，船公司、保险公司、商检机构等部门对国际惯例的不熟悉或误解和疏忽也会导致不符点。

再次，信用证本身的缺陷往往会引起致命的不符点。这包括几种情形：

1) 信用证含有软条款。软条款使出口商无法执行信用证，或不能获得信用证项下要求的单据。

2）信用证本身含糊或自相矛盾。

3）信用证修改也有可能导致不符点。这类不符点经常是由于开证行和受益人疏于对修改内容以外条款的审查引起的。

4）信用证条款与实际操作有冲突。

最后，受益人在经营过程中的脱节也是形成不符点的一个重要原因。

信用证只是一种结算工具，对于开证申请人来讲，旨在规范受益人及时履行合同，而就信用证受益人本身而言，在规定的时间内按质量备货、生产、发运显得尤为重要，单据的一些缺陷可以修改，但由于公司经营造成的失误，如货物无法在规定时间内产出，产生短装、船期赶不上，则无法挽回。信用证规定要求某部门出具的检验证书，公司因疏忽导致出运前未获得检验证书的情况，则往往无法更改。

Task 5　Asking for Extension of L/C

Preparing

Relative Reading

When Asking for Extension of an L/C, It Often Consists of the Following Parts.

1) In the opening sentences express your thanks for the L/C you received and give a detailed description about it.

2) Give the reasons why you have to ask for the extension of the L/C.

3) Put forward the detailed requirements of shipment and validity extension.

4) Express your appreciation for the extension and make sure you will make prompt shipment.

Explaining the Necessity of L/C Extension.

We have received your letter of July 7th and regret to learn that you are unable to extend the subject L/C.

As is known to you, there is only one vessel sailing for your port each month and it usually leaves here in the first half of a month. So far as we known, the only vessel available this month will leave here in a day or two and the deadline for booking shipping space is long past, therefore it is impossible for us to ship the goods this month, and we would ask you to do your best to extend the L/C as requested in our letter of June 30th.

✓ Lead In — Dialogues

Bob: Lisa, I would like to talk about the L/C No. 101.

Lisa: Okay, Bob. What's up?

Bob: You know because of the super typhoon "plum blossoms", it's hard for us to book space recently. But the letter of credit expires on 15th August.

Lisa: Oh, I learnt of the serious influence of "Plum blossom".

Bob: Yeah, so I wonder if you can grant us an extension of 2 weeks.

Lisa: It seems we have no other choices. The validity of the L/C will be extended to 30th August.

Bob: Great! Thank you for your understanding. Really appreciate it.

Performing

✓ Text

Sample 1　Asking for Extension of L/C

Dear Sirs,

L/C No. 109 5M/T Frozen Goat Meat

We thank you for your L/C No. 109 for the captioned goods. We are sorry that owing to some delay on the part of our suppliers, we are unable to get the goods ready before the end of this month. So we write to you asking for an extension.

It is expected that the consignment will be ready for shipment in the early part of June and we are arranging to ship it on S. S "Red Star" sailing from Dalian on June 10.

We are looking forward to receiving your extension of the above L/C, thus enabling us to effect shipment of the goods in question.

　　　　　　　　　　　　　　　　　　　　　　　　　　　Yours faithfully,

Sample 2　Asking for Extension of L/C

Dear Sirs,

We are sorry to report that in spite of our effort, we are unable to guarantee shipment by the agreed date due to a strike at our factory. We are afraid that your L/C will be expired before shipment. Therefore, please explain our situation to your customers and secure their consent to extend the L/C to Sept. 30.

　　　　　　　　　　　　　　　　　　　　　　　　　　　Sincerely,

Situation 5　Terms of Payment

Sample 3　A Favorable Reply to the Letter Asking for Extension of L/C

Gentlemen,

We received your letter today and have informed our customers of your situation. As requested, we have instructed the Beijing City Commercial Bank to extend the L/C up to and including September 30. Please keep us abreast of any new development.

　　　　　　　　　　　　　　　　　　　　　　　　　　　　　　Sincerely,

Notes

1) supplier　*n.* 供应商
2) extension　*n.* （信用证的）延展
3) consignment　*n.* 交托的物品，货物
4) in question　在考虑中的；在议论中的，上述的
5) in spite of　虽然；尽管……仍
   e.g. I went out in spite of the rain.
   　　　尽管下雨我还是出去了。
6) the agreed date　商定的日期
   agreed　已经过协议的，同意的
7) expire　*v.* 期满，终止
   e.g. My membership in the club has expired.
   　　　我的俱乐部会员资格已期满。
8) secure their consent to　获得他们的同意做……
   consent　*n.* 同意；应允；允许
   e.g. Mary's parents secured their consent to her marriage.
   　　　玛丽的父母不同意她的婚事。
9) extend the L/C up to　把信用证延展到……
10) keep abreast of　赶得上；与时俱进
    e.g. we have to keep abreast of the times in science.
    　　　我们必须在科学方面与时俱进。

Practicing

I. Translate the following expressions into English.

供应商　　　　　　　　　　　与时俱进
交托的物品，货物　　　　　　在考虑中的
虽然　　　　　　　　　　　　商定的日期
期满，终止　　　　　　　　　赶得上
获得他们的同意做……　　　　把信用证延展到……

II. Fill in the blanks.

1. We trust you will pay our draft _____ presentation.

2. Please pay special attention _____ this point.

3. We shall be glad if you will agree _____ ship the goods to us _____ before on cash against documents basis.

4. We hope that you will accommodate us _____ this respect and continue supplying us with enamelware _____ the same basis.

5. We would like to know something _____ the styles prevailing at your end.

6. We hope this will not involve you _____ any great inconvenience.

7. Mr. White refers to do business _____ D/A terms.

8. Please let us have your price list _____ your enamelware.

III. Translate the following sentences into Chinese.

1. We regret that we could not ship the goods by an April vessel because of the delay of your L/C. We request that you make up the extension of the L/C as soon as possible.

2. We request that you extend the shipping date to December 30, 2017 and the credit validity to January 15, 2018. Please send us your reply as soon as possible.

3. We write to you asking for an extension of the shipping date for one month.

4. We earnestly hope that you will extend the letter of credit to the 30th of this month.

5. Documents must be presented within 15 days after the date of issuance of the transport documents but within the validity of this letter of credit.

IV. Writing practice.

1. Write a letter stating the following points.

   1) You cannot ship the order because you haven't got the relevant L/C.

   2) Require the time of shipment to be extended to the end of October.

   3) Require the validity of the L/C to be extended to Nov. 15.

   4) You must receive their L/C amendment before Sept. 30.

2. Write a letter about asking for extension of L/C (open).

Supplement

✓ Supplementary Reading

1. Letter: An Unfavorable Reply to the Letter Asking for Extension of L/C

Dear Sirs,

L/C NSW 6180

We have received your letter of June 30th requesting us to extend the above L/C to the

31st of August and the 15th of September for shipment and negotiation respectively.

We are quite aware of the conditions set forth in S/C 89STX-5491 that the goods ordered could be shipped in July if the covering L/C reached you on the 15th of June at the latest. However, as we had to go through the necessary formalities of applying for the relevant import license, we could not open the L/C earlier. The import license is granted on June 17 and is valid only up to the 31st of July.

We are willing to do whatever we can to cooperate with you, but as the present import regulations do not allow any extension of license, we regret having to say that it is beyond our ability to meet your request to extend the above L/C.

Please do your best to ship the goods in time and we thank you for your cooperation.

Yours faithfully,

2. Example Sentences

1) 由于本月没有贵方港口的直达轮，我方要求延长信用证有效期至 5 月 31 日。

   As there is no direct steamer to your port this month, please extend the validity of L/C to May 31.

2) 由于你方信用证装运期与有效期相同，请按惯例将信用证有效期延展十五天。

   As the time of shipment and validity in your L/C are the same, please extend the validity of the L/C for 15 days according to practice.

3) 我方已根据贵方第 308 号信用证条款，将全套清洁已装船海运提单连同其他单据提交中国银行福州分行。

   According to the clauses of L/C No. 308, we have presented full set of clean "on board" ocean bill of lading and other documents to the Bank of China, Fuzhou Branch。

4) 关于第 689 号信用证，我方已指示开证行将装运期和有效期分别延到 9 月 30 日和 10 月 15 日。

   As regards L/C No. 689, we have instructed the issuing bank to extend the date of shipment and the validity in L/C to September 30 and October 15 respectively.

5) 经核对信用证条款，我方遗憾地发现你方信用证要求 10 月份装运，但我方合约规定 11 月份装运，因此，务请把装运期和议付期分别展至 11 月 30 日和 12 月 15 日。

   After checking the stipulations in the L/C, we regret to find that your L/C calls for October shipment. But the contract stipulates November shipment, you are requested to extend the date of shipment and the validity for negotiation of L/C to Nov. 30 and Dec. 15 respectively.

 Knowledge Link

☆UCP600 的新内涵

首先，可撤销信用证的提法被取消。在实务操作中，当事人开立的都是不可撤销的信用证，所以，可撤销信用证不再有存在的必要。

其次，UCP600出现了一个新定义"承付"。"承付"概括了在即期付款、延期付款和承兑信用证条件下，开证行、保兑行或指定行除议付外的其他向受益人进行支付的行为。同时，UCP600对"议付"的定义也进行了修订，争议颇大的"给付对价"的说法被删除，在新条款中被称为"购买"，明确了议付是对票据和单据的"购买"，属于对受益人的预付或承诺预付。

最后，信用证业务一旦开立是独立于合同的。信用证业务精神在UCP500里就是如此表述的："单证相符、单单不得互不一致。"UCP600的精神表明：即使在单证间也不要求"等同"，仅要求"不得矛盾"，这样比过去单单之间"不得互不一致"的说法更体现了审单标准宽松化的倾向。从这点上来讲，UCP600的最大作用就是扶持信用证的使用，规范信用证业务的实施。

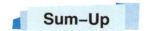

Sum-Up

The following sentences are usually used in terms of payment.

1. It's convenient to make payment in pound sterling.
   用英镑付款较方便。

2. We can't accept payment on deferred terms.
   我们不能接受延期付款。

3. This is the normal terms of payment in international business.
   这是国际贸易中惯用的付款方式。

4. We'll not pay until shipping documents for the goods reaches us.
   见不到货物装船单据，我们不付款。

5. Please protect our draft on presentation.
   请见票即付。

6. Your draft will be honoured on presentation.
   你方的汇票见票即付。

7. We've drawn a clean draft on you for the value of this sample shipment.
   我们已经开出光票向你方索取这批样货的价款。

8. We've drawn on you for payment of the invoice amounting to USD 20,000.
   我们已经按照发票金额20,000美元向你方开出了汇票。

9. We'll draw on you by our documentary draft at sight on collection basis.
   我们将按托收方式向你方开出即期跟单汇票。

10. The draft was discounted in New York.
    汇票已经在纽约贴现。

11. We'll agree to change the terms of payment from L/C at sight to D/P at sight.
    我们同意将即期信用证付款方式改为即期付款交单。

Situation 5　Terms of Payment

12. We can do the business on 60 days D/P basis.
    我们可以按 60 天付款交单的方式进行交易。
13. As a special sign of encouragement, we'll consider accepting payment by D/P at this sales-purchasing stage.
    在此推销阶段，我们将考虑接受付款交单方式以资鼓励。
14. I suppose D/P or D/A should be adopted as the mode of payment this time.
    我建议这次用付款交单或承兑交单方式来付款。
15. L/C at sight is normal for our exports to France.
    我们向法国出口一般使用即期信用证付款。
16. Our terms of payment is confirmed and irrevocable letter of credit.
    我们的付款条件是保兑的不可撤销的信用证。
17. For payment, we require 100% value, irrevocable L/C in our favour with partial shipment allowed clause available by draft at sight.
    我们的付款方式是不可撤销的、允许分批装运，并以我方为抬头人的足额信用证，见票即付。
18. It's expensive to open an L/C, because we need to put a deposit in the bank.
    开证得交押金，因此花费较大。
19. Your refusal to amend the L/C is equivalent to cancellation of the order.
    你们拒绝修改信用证就等于取消订单。
20. We find that the following two points do not conform to the contract.
    我们发现信用证条款中有两点与合同不符。
21. We write to you asking for an extension of the shipping date for one month.
    兹去信要求将装运期延长一个月。
22. We earnestly hope that you will extend the letter of credit to the 30th of this month.
    我们诚挚地希望贵方能将信用证的有效期延长至本月 30 日。
23. What is the mode of payment you wish to employ?
    您希望用什么方式付款?

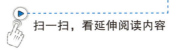 扫一扫，看延伸阅读内容

Situation 06

Shipment and Insurance

📝 Objectives

1) To be able to translate and write a letter of packing requirements.
2) To be able to translate and write a letter of shipment.
3) To be able to translate and write a letter of insurance.

📝 Introduction

After a contract is confirmed, the exporter will prepare the goods for shipment. Shipment covers rather a wide range of work: packing, confirming shipment clause, booking shipping space, chartering a vessel, amending shipping terms, etc.

The sellers should arrange the shipment under terms of CIF or CFR, while on FOB basis this will be arranged by the importer. Of course, since the importer is so far away and cannot conveniently make such arrangements he may ask the exporter to do it on behalf.

Before the goods are shipped on board, they must be packed in different ways to avoid being damaged or stolen. When the goods are ready for shipment and the carrying vessel is ready, it is the duty of the exporter to see to it that the goods are placed on board the carrying vessel, following which the exporter will get from the shipping company a bill of lading (B/L) and give the importer shipping advice.

Insurance is also a key issue in foreign trade. In international trade, the transportation of goods from seller to the buyer is generally over a long distance and it has to go through the procedures of transit, loading and unloading, storage, etc. During the process, it is quite possible that the goods will encounter various kinds of perils and sometimes suffer losses. In order to protect the goods against possible loss in case of such perils, the buyer or the seller before the transportation of the goods usually applies to an insurance company for insurance covering the goods in transit against these risks in accordance with the mode of transport used, the nature of the goods and the insurance terms stipulated in the contract.

Main Points of Shipment

1) Referring to the relative commodity, contract or order.
2) a. Giving packing instructions (for a letter giving details of packing requirements).
   b. Asking for early shipment and giving the reason (for a letter urging shipment).
   c. Proposing new shipment terms and giving reason (for a letter asking to amend shipment terms).
   d. Advising shipment and giving the details (for a letter advising shipment of goods).
3) Expecting cooperation, early reply or early shipment.

Main Points of Insurance

1) Referring to the relative goods, contract or shipment.
2) Introducing the insurance and usual practice.
3) Stating the details of insurance such as coverage, premium, amount insured and extra premium.
4) Expressing your wishes.

Task 1   Packing Requirements

Preparing

✓ Relative Reading

1. What is the Purpose of Packing?

Packing is of great importance in foreign trade. It may be appropriately said that packing is to goods as what clothing is to man. The ultimate purpose of packing is to keep the transported goods in prefect condition with nothing missing on arrival. Good packing must be able to stand the roughest transportation.

2. What are the Two Styles of Packing?

Packing can be divided into transport packing (usually known as outer packing) and sales packing (usually known as inner packing). Transport packing is done mainly to keep the goods safe and sound during transportation. It must not only be soiled enough to prevent the packed goods from any damage, but also pilferage-proof, easy to store, convenient to load and unload. Sales packing is done mainly to push sales.

3. Features of Packing

durable and beautiful

easy to handle

suitable for long distance shipment

proof against damage / water /shake

standardized

4. Appearance and Packaging of Packing

small and exquisite

attractive

suitable for window display

facilitate marketing in supermarket

5. Factors Which Influence the Nature of Packing

value of the goods

nature of the transit

nature of the cargo

compliance with customers' statutory requirements

resale value of packing materials, general fragility of cargo

variation in temperature during the course of the transit

ease of handling and stowage

insurance acceptance conditions

cost of packing

✓ Lead In — Dialogues

The following is a talk between Mr. Anderson (A) and Mr. Wang (B) about packing for fragile goods.

A: You know chinaware is fragile and needs strong and careful packing. Could you tell me what kind of packing you plan to use for this consignment of goods?

B: Cartons. Is that OK?

A: I'm afraid that won't do. I once bought a lot of chinaware from another company and when the consignment arrived, I found some of the cartons broken and the goods inside damaged. It was a really terrible experience. So I don't think cartons are strong enough for fragile goods.

B: But we'll use metal straps to reinforce the cartons, and they'll be handled with care. We always pay particular attention to the safety of packing. Please don't worry.

A: But I don't want to take any chances. What about using wooden cases instead?

B: We'll use wooden cases if you insist. But wooden cases are much heavier than cartons, and you'll have to pay the extra packing fee.

A: We have to protect the goods from any possible damage during transit by using wooden cases. A little more expense hardly matters.

B: Okay, we'll pack the goods according to your instructions.

A: Thank you. There's still one last thing I'd like to mention here. Please don't forget to stencil warning marks like "fragile", "handle with care" and other relevant marks on the wooden cases.

B: Of course, if it will reassure you, we'll do that too.

Performing

Sample 1 Packing Instruction

Dear Sir or Madam,

We've received your E-mail of October 9, regarding our trial order of 20 cases of machine parts.

Please see to it that as machine parts are susceptible to shocks, they must be wrapped in soft materials and firmly packed in seaworthy cases to avoid any movement inside the cases. The unvarnished ferrous metal parts should be well greased to prevent rusting.

We trust that you can meet the above requirements and thank you in advance for your cooperation.

Yours sincerely,
Ken
ABC Co. Ltd.

Sample 2 Shipping Marks

Dear Sirs,

Enclosed is our Contract No. 3322 covering 6,000 "Crystal" Transistors, Model O12 with our countersignature.

We'd like you to have the goods packed in cardboard cartons, two dozen of each. Please stencil the shipping mark on the outer packing as follows:

Meanwhile, indicative marks as "Handle With Care" should be added beside the shipping mark as any negligence in packing and transportation may cause unexpected trouble and expenses.

We are looking forward to receiving your shipping advice with keen interest.

Yours faithfully,

John Smith

Sample 3 Packing Requirements

Dear Sirs,

We regret to inform you that of the 100 cardboard cartons of screws you shipped to Istanbul on 28 January, eight were delivered damaged, of course, through no fault of yours.

We are writing you about the packing of these screws, in order to avoid the similar incident, we feel necessary to clarify the concrete stipulation for our future dealings.

The packing for Istanbul should be in wooden cases of 112 pounds net, each containing 7 pounds x 16 packets. For Jeddah, we would like you to have the goods packed in double gunny bags of 50 kilos each. As for the Calcutta market, our buyers prefer 25 kilo cardboard cartons.

Please let us know whether these requirements could be met.

Yours faithfully,

Notes

1) see to   务必……，注意……
    see to sth.   务必做到
    see to it that…   注意，务必，保证

2) be susceptible to   易受……影响的，易于……
    e. g. Water proof lining are susceptible to protect the shipment from moisture.
           防水衬里易于防潮。

3) be wrapped in   被包（裹）在……里面

4) **pack** v. put things into a box, bundle, bag, etc.   包装

be packed in... 用……装

e. g. The commodity should be packed in polybags.

商品必须用塑料袋包装。

be packed in ... of ... each 被包装在每个……中

e. g. The shoes are packed in cartons of 30 pairs each.

鞋用纸箱包装，每箱30双。

be packed in..., ... to ... 被包装在每个……个

e. g. Our scissors are packed in boxes of 20 pieces each, and 100 boxes to a wooden case. 剪刀用纸盒包装，每盒20个，100盒装一木箱。

5) The unvarnished ferrous metal parts should be well greased to prevent rusting.

未涂漆的含铁金属零件应涂上润滑油，以免生锈。

6) cardboard cartons 纸板箱

7) stencil *v.* print a pattern or words 刷唛

e. g. The package is stenciled with "DG London". 这个包装刷着"DG 伦敦"字样。

8) negligence *n.* carelessness 疏忽，粗心大意

e. g. Any damage due to negligence of the packing will result in the losses.

包装的任何疏忽将导致损失。

Practicing

I. Translate the following expressions into English.

小心轻放   务必，确保
指示性标志   警告性标志
易受……影响   唛头
贸易争端   适于海运的包装
便于装运   包装要求

II. Choose the best answer to complete each of the following sentences.

1. Women's leather gloves are packed _____ cartons _____ 100 pairs each.

   A. to, for   B. of, for   C. in, of   D. with, of

2. As requested, we will have the goods _____ in wooden cases, but you have to bear the extra _____ charges.

   A. packing, repacked   B. repacked, packing
   C. packing, packing   D. package, repacked

3. We sincerely hope the goods under your Order No. 123 will reach you _____.

   A. in good conditions   B. in the good conditions

    C. in a good condition   D. in good condition

4. Our clients prefer small _____.

   A. packer   B. packing   C. package   D. packaging

5. The goods should be packed in _____ plastic bags.

   A. five ply   B. five plies   C. five-ply   D. five-plies

6. _____ is advisable for you to strengthen the case with double straps.

   A. It   B. This   C. That   D. The

7. Our cotton shirts are packed _____ boxes, 200 boxes _____ a carton.

   A. with, to   B. in, to   C. in, in   D. with, in

8. The package is stenciled _____ "Handle with Care".

   A. with   B. in   C. of   D. to

9. We have made _____ clear that the goods should be packed in cartons.

   A. them   B. this   C. which   D. it

10. We found that nearly 20% of the _____ had been broken, obviously attributed to improper _____.

   A. packages, packing   B. packet, packages

   C. packing, packages   D. package, packing

III. Translate the following sentences into Chinese.

1. Normally, packing charge is included in the contract price.

2. The machines must be well protected against dampness, moisture and shock.

3. Only by the end of the next month the goods can be packed ready for delivery.

4. Taking into consideration the transport at your end, we have especially reinforced our packing.

5. A packing that catches the eye will help us push the sales.

IV. Writing practice.

1. Write a letter stating the following points.

你是买方，现在给卖方写信，说明你们指定的运输标志：在一个菱形内写上你方公司名称缩写DGH，菱形下面标明箱数和目的港。另说明卖方遵照你方要求行事的必要性。

2. Write a letter of complaining about the packing condition.

Situation 6　Shipment and Insurance

Supplement

✓ Supplementary Reading

1. Letter 1: Packing

Dear Sir or Madam,

　　We are pleased to inform you that your order of 8,000 bottles of grape wine is ready. We shall pack them in cartons because cartons are comparatively light and compact, more convenient to handle.

　　Furthermore, cartons will prevent pilferage, for the traces of pilferage will be more in evidence. We have enclosed a photo of packed sample for you.

　　We hope you will accept our carton packing and assure you of our sincere cooperation. Please let us know if you have special requirement.

Yours sincerely,
Alan Brown

2. Letter 2: Reply to the Above

Dear Sir or Madam,

　　Thank you for your E-mail of May 8 about the packing details. I immediately approached our clients about the packing. After our repeated explanation, they insist on packing the grape wine in wooden cases instead of cartons. The reason is that the cartons used are not seaworthy.

　　We think you will understand that our frank statements are made for our mutual benefits as packing is a sensitive subject, which often leads to trade disputes.

　　Kindly let us know whether the requirement could be met.

Yours sincerely,
Eric
BCD Co. Ltd.

3. Two Types of Packing

Transportation packing or outer packing.

4. The Purpose of Outer Packing

To protect goods from damaging or stealing.

To facilitate transporting, loading, unloading and carrying.

To economize freight cost, lower possible customs duties and insurance premium.

5. The Purpose of Inner Packing

To protect goods.

To help customers identify goods.

To make goods appeal to customers.

6. Outer Packing and Inner Packing

Outer packing is used for the convenience of protecting and transporting goods. Inner packing, also known as small packing or immediate packing, is designed for the promotion of sales.

The goods should be packed in a way according to the importer's instructions or the trade custom, without violating the import country's regulations on outer packing material, length and weight, or going against the import country's social customs and national preference for inner packing colors and designs, etc.

To facilitate the identification of goods, the outer packing must be marked clearly with identifying symbols and numbers which should be the same as indicated in the commercial invoice, the consular invoice, the bill of lading and the other shipping documents.

7. Packing Marks

While packing is to serve the purpose of protecting the goods, marking is to give information about the goods inside.

8. What Marks are Usually Done on Export Packages?

1) the consignee's own distinctive marks (including the name of the port of destination).

2) Shipping marks: indicate where the products are made, where the products are shipped, and the Order No. of the goods and the identity of the goods.

3) Indicative and warning marks: remind and warn the relevant persons to pay attention and ensure the safety of both operators and goods.

✓ Knowledge Link

☆ 包装标志的分类

包装标志是包装上不可或缺的重要部分，一般分为三类：

1. 运输标志

运输标志即通常所说的唛头，它一般包括四部分：1) 收货人缩写或代号；2) 参考号、如订单号、发票号码、合同号码等；3) 目的地；4) 件数。

2. 指示性标志

它用来提示人们在装卸、搬运、保管过程中应该注意的事项，一般由简洁明了的文字或图案组成。

常见的外包装指示性标志有：

This side up	此面朝上
Handle with care	小心轻放
Keep from moisture	防潮
No hook	勿用钓具
Keep dry	保持干燥
Keep cool	保持阴凉

3. 警告性标志

它又被称为危险品包装标志，一般用作某些易燃易爆物品、化学物品、有毒物品、放射性物品等特种物品的运输标志，以警示人们做好防护措施。

☆ 部分国家对于包装的特殊规定

新西兰禁止进口农产品的包装使用稻草、麦草、干草、土壤、泥灰等做材料。

希腊规定出口到该国的产品必须在包装上用希腊文注明公司名称、产品名称、数量、质量等。

利比亚禁止进口产品的包装使用猪和女性人体等图案。

德国禁止进口产品的包装使用类似纳粹或军团等图案。

Task 2 Shipment

Preparing

Relative Reading

Introduction

Shipment is one of the indispensable terms of a contract. It involves transport which is an important part in international business. In practice, shipment involves such procedures:

1) clearing the goods through the customs.
2) booking space or chartering a ship.
3) completing shipping documents.
4) dispatching/sending shipping advice.

Terms of Shipment Contain

Time of shipment; ports of shipment and destination; time of loading; shipping documents, etc.

Time of shipment: refers to a period of time or a deadline for a consignment/shipment/parcel/goods to be loaded on board (of) a vessel.

The Points Regarding Transport are as Follows

1) Means of conveyance (运送方式): by road or rail, by sea or air or combined transport: a road-sea-rail carriage/conveyance.

2) Forms of carriage contracts are consignment note (托运单) or airway bill (航空提单或货运单) when goods are transported by road /rail or air; sea transport involves chartering a vessel/ship (租船) or booking shipping space (订舱), thus contracts signed between the ship owner and the shipper may appear in the form of either a charter party (租船契约) or a bill of lading (海运提单).

Applicable Structure for Letters on Shipment

1) Open the letter in a positive way. Especially when negative information is conveyed, great care should be taken.

2) Explain the problem in great detail to try to persuade the reader into accepting the request or to make the reader fully aware of the request.

3) Close the letter by expressing good wishes to encourage the reader to cooperate.

✔ Lead In — Dialogues

Miss Yang (A) is having a talk with Mr. Wilson (B), discussing the details about shipment.

A: When we negotiate the shipment, we'd better put down the specific date. It would be advisable not to include such terms as "prompt shipment" or "immediate delivery" in our contract.

B: Absolutely. What would you say to prompt shipment by the end of October?

A: I'm afraid we can't make it. You see, from now to the end of October, is only one and a half months. As far as I know, shipping space for the line has been fully booked up to mid-October.

B: I'm sure you must know what prompt shipment means to us. Long sea voyage, the customs formalities and the flow through the marketing channels to retailers would take at least 40 days. There is no time to lose.

Situation 6   Shipment and Insurance

A: Well. It has always been our wish to satisfy our clients. The problem now is to sort out the quickest possible way to ship the goods for the selling season.

B: Since there is no shipping space on direct steamers, will you please find some other way out?

A: It has just occurred to me that if we could arrange for transshipment in Singapore, things will become much better, as there are more frequent sailings to Europe there.

B: Even if transshipment space to Europe from Singapore is available, it will also add considerably to the expenses and risks.

A: To you, time is crucial. I think it is worth trying if transshipment via Singapore will help you catch the seasonal demand.

B: I fully agree with you. That being the case, I suggest we note under the shipment clause "shipment is to be made by the first available vessel in October, with transshipment via Singapore allowed".

A: That's no problem.

B: I understand that the buyer should, in advance, inform the seller of the shipping instructions.

A: You are right. And the seller should give the buyer the shipping advice as soon as shipment is effected.

B: I agree to these terms. Miss Yang, I'm impressed greatly by your considerate cooperation.

A: It's my pleasure. Have you any more questions on this deal?

B: Not for the time being.

Performing

✓ Text

Sample 1   Urging Shipment

Dear Sirs,

Our Order No. 6767 Covering 600 Electric Fans

As it is more than two weeks since we opened a letter of credit in your favor, we wish to draw your attention to its expiration date — 31 January.

Since the season is approaching, our buyers are badly in need of the goods. We would like you to effect shipment as soon as possible, thus enabling them to catch the brisk season in business.

We would like to emphasize that any delay in shipping our booked order will undoubtedly

involve us in trouble.

Please look into the matter and give us your definite reply without further delay.

Yours faithfully,

Sample 2 Asking for Partial Shipment

Dear Sirs,

We have received your letter of May 25, 2017 requesting us to ship all the 40 sets of juice extractor in one lot. Unfortunately we are unable to comply with your wishes.

When we ordered these juice extractors it was clearly stated that shipment would be effected in August. If you desire earlier delivery, we can only make a partial shipment of twenty sets in July and the remaining twenty in August. We hope this arrangement will be agreeable to you. Should this be so, please amend the covering L/C to allow partial shipment.

Please let us have your confirmation immediately so that we can request the manufacturers to expedite delivery.

Yours faithfully,

Sample 3 Shipping Instruction

Dear Sirs,

We are glad to learn from your letter of 25 March that you have booked our order for two Model 780 Machines. Our confirmation of order will be sent to you in a few days.

Since the purchase is made on FOB basis, please arrange shipment of the goods from Liverpool on a ship reserved by us. As soon as the shipping space is booked, we shall advise you of the name of the ship. For further instructions, please contact our forwarding agent, ABC Company, Liverpool, who has been taking care of shipments from you.

As some parts of the machines are susceptible to shock, the machines must be packed in seaworthy cases capable of withstanding rough handling. The bright metal parts should be protected from water dampness in transit by a coating of grease that will keep out dampness.

We trust that the above instructions are clear to you and that shipment will give the users entire satisfaction.

Yours faithfully,

Situation 6 Shipment and Insurance

Notes

1) the sales season 销售旺季
   come into season 上市
   dead/ dull/ off season 萧条季节，淡季
   high/ brisk season 旺季

2) approach v. to come near or nearer, as in space or time 接近，靠近
   e.g. As the sales season is approaching, please arrange shipment as soon as possible. 销售旺季即将来临，请尽快发货。

3) badly in need   in urgent need 急需

4) shipment n. 装船，装运的货物
   部分常见的装船表示法：
   shipment during January 或 January shipment 一月份装船
   shipment not later than Jan. 31 装运时间不迟于 1 月 31 日；或 shipment on or before Jan. 31 在 1 月 31 日或之前装船
   shipment during ... in two lots 在……（时间）分两批装船
   in three monthly shipments 分三个月装运
   immediate shipment 立即装运
   prompt shipment 即期装运
   partial shipment 分批装运
   make/ effect/ arrange shipment 办理装船
   shipments within 30 days after receipt of L/C 收到信用证后 30 天装运

5) delay n. 延迟，拖延
   delay in (后接动名词)
   delay of (后接延迟若干时间)
   without further delay 尽早
   e.g. Excuse us for delay in answering your letter. 来信迟复为歉。

6) juice extractor 榨汁机

7) confirmation n. 确认，批准
   full confirmation 完全确认
   in confirmation of （以便）证实……
   sales confirmation 售货确认书
   purchase confirmation 购货确认书

8) expedite v. 加快，加速
   e.g. Shipment is ready, please expedite credit.
   船已装完，请速开立信用证。

Practicing

I. Translate the following expressions into Chinese.

shipping documents   port of discharge

port of loading   immediate shipment

brisk season   partial shipment

sailing date   in four equal monthly shipments

purchase confirmation   full confirmation

II. Fill in the blanks with proper forms of given words.

| load | ship | involve | sail | compensate |

1. You may be assured that all _____ will be made by us.

2. The _____ company will be responsible for the damage in transit.

3. This transaction _____ only a small amount.

4. The ship is scheduled to _____ for Hong Kong on the 30 of this month.

5. We'd better have a brief talk about the _____ port.

III. Translate the following sentences into English.

1. 我们从船公司获悉，五月底前前往东京的舱位已订满，最早装运时间为 6 月 8 日。

2. 为赶上销售旺季，一旦收到我方开出的信用证，请立即安排装运。

3. 我想知道你们能否在九月份装运。

4. 若货物在装运期过期后装运，我们将拒收货物并保留索赔的权利。

5. 另一种方法就是我们将货物分批装运。

IV. Writing practice.

1. You have concluded a transaction of Samsung cell phones with a Korean businessman on FOB basis. Now write a letter to give shipping instruction and packing details as follows:

　1) 已经向中国远洋运输公司订妥舱位。

　2) 唛头要求如下：在外包装上刷上我公司的首字母缩写"HW"、目的港、订单号和箱号。

　3) 希望准时装船。

2. Write a letter about shipping advice（open）.

Situation 6　Shipment and Insurance

Supplement

✓ Supplementary Reading

1. Letter 1: Booking Shipping Containers

Dear Sirs,

We have 50 cases of medicines and chemical reagents at the above address ready for dispatch to any European main port, and shall be glad if you will arrange for your shipping container to collect them. Each case weighs 60 kgs.

As our client requires us to ship the goods not later than July 15, please quote us for a shipping container from Hong Kong to the above mentioned port before that deadline.

Your early quotation will be highly appreciated.

Yours faithfully,

2. Letter 2: Shipping Advice

Dear Sirs,

We are pleased to inform you that the following goods under our contract No. CC1200 have now been shipped by S. S. "Feng Qing" sailing tomorrow from Guangzhou to Sydney.

Order No. C120   10 Bales Grey Cotton Cloth
Order No. C135   10 Bales White Cotton Cloth

Copies of the relative shipping documents are enclosed, thus you may find no trouble in taking delivery of the goods when they arrive.

We hope this shipment will reach you in time and turn out to your entire satisfaction.

Yours faithfully,

3. Three Parties Involved in the Movement of the Goods

the consigner (发货人) — who sends the goods.
the carrier (承运人) — who carries them.
the consignee (收货人) — who receives them at the destination.

4. The Two Types of Ocean Shipping Services

In sea transport, there are two types of ocean shipping services: liners and tramps.

Liners sail on scheduled dates/times between a group of ports. But tramps, also called general traders, usually trade in various ports in search of cargo transportation business.

Once the goods are loaded on board a ship or placed under the control of the shipping company, or its agent, issues a bill of lading (B/L) to the shipper, usually the exporter, as a receipt for goods and evidence of contract of carriage between the shipping company and the shipper. The bill of lading is also an important document of title to the goods.

When the exporter finds it necessary to have a whole ship at his disposal for the carriage of goods, he charters a ship, that is to say, to hire a ship from the ship owner. The chartering of a ship can be on the basis of voyage, time or demise.

The contract between the ship owner and charterer, one who hires the ship, is known as the Charter Party.

Either a charter party or a bill of lading is a contract between the ship owner and the consignor (one who sends the goods).

5. Letters Regarding Shipment are Usually Written for the Following Purpose

To send shipping instructions and urge an early shipment (发送装运说明并敦促早日装运).

To amend shipping terms (修改装运条款).

To give shipping advice (发送装运通知).

To dispatch shipping documents (发送货运单据).

6. A Shipping Advice Usually Contains the Following Points

The date and number of bill of lading. (提单号码和日期)

The date and number of the contract. (合同号码和日期)

The names of commodities and their quality and value. (商品名称、质量及价值)

The name of the carrying vessel. (承运船只名称)

The name of the shipping port/loading port. (装货港口/卸货港口名称)

The estimated time of departure. (预定起航日期)

The name of the destination port. (目的港名称)

The estimated time of arrival. (预定到港日期)

A list of the relevant shipping documents. (货运单据列表)

Thanks for patronage. (感谢光顾)

7. A Letter of Shipment Usually Includes the following Points

Introduce the matter concerned, the shipment of goods under the given order.

Provide all the details of shipment that both parties concerns. If needed, they may be put in more than one paragraph.

State the response required from the recipient and you will take the action as a result.

Knowledge Link

☆ 交货与装运

交货是指卖方按照同买方约定的时间、地点和运输方式将合同规定的货物交付给买方或其代理人。装运一般是指将货物装上运输工具，它与交货是两个不同的概念。但是，在国际商务中，由于采用 FOB、CFR 和 CIF 三种价格术语，卖方只要根据合同的有关规定将货物装上船，取得提单，就算交货。提单签发日期即为交货日。因此，装运一词常被用来代替交货的概念。这种凭单交货被称为象征性交货。(实际交货是指货物运抵目的地，因而，装运时间与交货时间是并不一致的。) 凭单交货时，装运期和交货期是一致的。在买卖合同中，合理地规定装运期（交货期）是很重要的。

☆ 世界主要港口

1. European Main Ports 欧洲主要港口

Port of Rotterdam	鹿特丹港（荷兰）
Port of Hamburg	汉堡港（德国）
Port of London	伦敦港（英国）
Port of Antwerp	安特卫普港（比利时）
Port of Helsinki	赫尔辛基港（芬兰）
Port of Geneva	热那亚港（意大利）
Port of Marseille	马赛港（法国）

2. Asian Main Ports 亚洲主要港口

Port of Shanghai	上海港（中国）
Port of Hong Kong	香港港口（中国）
Port of Bussan	釜山港（韩国）
Port of Kobe	神户港（日本）
Port of Dubai	迪拜港（阿联酋）
Port of Mumbai	孟买港（印度）
Port of Singapore Authority	新加坡港（新加坡）

3. American Main Ports 美洲主要港口

Port of Toronto	多伦多港（加拿大）
Port Authority of New York and New Jersey	纽约-新泽西港（美国）
Port of Mazatlan	马萨特兰港（墨西哥）
Port of Rio de Janeiro	里约热内卢港（巴西）

Task 3   Insurance

Preparing

Relative Reading

Background Information

The organization of Marine Insurance took great steps forward with the formation and development of an insurance market on Lombard Street in London, England and subsequently — since 1769 — Lloyds of London.

Today, Lloyds still plays a prominent role in Marine Insurance.

The first American insurer was Insurance Company of North America（北美洲保险公司）(now CNA, one of the companies that writes insurance for David G. Sayles Insurance Services), formed in 1794. CNA has operated continuously since that time, and remains an important market for marine as well as other forms of property and casualty insurance.

Definition of Insurance

Insurance is a contract whereby one party, in consideration of a premium paid, undertakes to indemnify the other party against loss from certain perils or risks to which the subject matter insured may be exposed to.

It is customary to insure goods sold for export against the risks of the journey.

In international trade, the transaction of goods from the seller to the buyer is generally over a long distance by air, by land or by sea and has to go through the procedures of loading, unloading and storing. During this process, it is quite possible that the goods will encounter various kinds of risks and sometimes suffer losses.

In order to protect the goods against possible loss in case of such risks, the buyers or sellers before the transportation of the goods usually apply to an insurance company for insurance covering the goods in transit.

The Premium

Charge for the insurance policy is calculated according to the risks involved. A policy which protects the holder against limited risks/which covers limited coverages charges a low

Situation 6 Shipment and Insurance

premium, and policy which protects against a large number of risks /which covers many coverages charges a high premium.

The Insurance Value

It is calculated as: cost of goods + amount of freight + insurance premium + a percentage of the total sum to represent a reasonable profit on sale of the goods.

Structure for Letters Concerning Insurance

1) State which kind of insurance is desired and provide the reader with convincing and specific reasons.

2) Put forward the problem of insurance in a positive way.

3) Express expectations for an early reply or cooperation.

✓ Lead In — Dialogues

Mr. Lee (A), an importer from USA, is having talk with Mr. Ma (B) on insurance.

A: Mr. Ma, I'd like to take several minutes of you to discuss some insurance problems with you, if you don't mind.

B: Of course not.

A: I'd like to know what kind of insurance you can provide on the terms of CIF?

B: We always provide With Particular Average (WPA).

A: Could you cover particular average, like SRCC, Risk of Leakage or Risk of Breakage?

B: For these additional coverage, we only insure according to the customers' requirements.

A: So should the extra premium incurred be for the buyer's account.

B: Of course. According to the international practice, we usually do not insure against additional coverage unless it is required by the buyer.

A: I see. What percent of invoice value do you always insure for based on CIF term?

B: We usually insure for 110% of the invoice value.

A: But some of our customers would like to have the insurance covered at 130% of the invoice value. Do you think that can be done?

B: I think so, but please note that our insurance coverage is usually for 110% of the invoice value, not for 130%. Thus the extra premium should be borne by the buyer.

A: That's understood.

Performing

Sample 1   Details of Insurance

Dear Sirs,

We have for acknowledgement your fax of June 20 in regard to insurance.

In reply, we are pleased to advise you of the following:

We generally cover insurance WPA and War Risk if no definite instructions have been received from our clients. If you desire to cover All Risks, such coverage can be arranged at a slightly higher premium.

For your information, the present rate being charged by the People's Insurance Company of China for the 10,000 metric tons of Chinese Rice against All Risks including War Risk from Shanghai to Lagos is 1% subject to PICC clauses. If you find the above-mentioned rate acceptable, please inform us immediately.

We agree to your request for covering insurance for 130% of the invoice value, but the premium for the difference between 130% and 110% of the invoice value should be for your account.

We trust the above information will serve your purpose and await your further news.

Yours respectfully,

Sample 2   Importer Asking Exporter to Cover Insurance

Dear Sir or Madam,

We wish to refer you to our Order No. 123 for 1,000 cases of toys, from which you will see that this order is placed on CFR basis.

In order to save time and simplify procedures, we now desire to have shipment insured at your end. We shall be pleased if you will arrange to insure the goods on our behalf against All Risks for 110% of the full invoice value.

We thank you for your cooperation in advance.

Yours sincerely,

Sample 3   Application for Insurance Against Leather Goods

Dear Sirs,

We shall shortly be making regular shipments of leather goods to Vancouver, Canada, by approved ships and shall be glad if you will issue an A R marine insurance policy for, say, USD 70,000 to cover these shipments from our warehouse at the above address to the port of destination.

All goods will be packed in wooden cases and dispatched by rail to Tianjing.

Yours faithfully,

Notes

1) insurance *n.* 保险

    arrange/ effect/ provide/ take out/ cover/ attend to insurance 投保，办理保险

    insurance agent 保险代理人

    insurance amount 保险金额

    insurance broker 保险经纪人

    insurance coverage 保险范围

    insure *v.* 投保（后接货物或险别）

    常用的表达方式：insure…（货物）for…（金额）with…（保险公司）against…（险别）

    e.g. We usually insure shipments with the PICC for the invoice value plus 10% against All Risks.

    按照惯例，我们将按发票金额加成10%向中国人民保险公司投保一切险。

2) premium *n.* the amount paid for an insurance policy 保险费

    premium rate 保险费率

    premium rebate 保险费回扣

3) cover *v.* 投保

    cover the goods against… 投保……险别

    cover the insurance with… 向……投保

4) for 130% of the invoice value 按发票金额的130%

5) for your account   to be borne by you 由你方承担

6) save time and simplify procedures 节约时间和简化程序

7) at your end/on your side 在你处

Practicing

I. Translate the following expressions into English.

保险范围   保险金额

保险费   保险费率

一切险   水渍险

平安险	中国人民保险公司
保险单	保险凭证

II. Complete the following letter with proper words.

Dear Sirs,

  _____ reply, we would like to _____ you that most of our clients are _____ their orders with us on CIF _____. This will _____ their time and simplify procedures. May we suggest that your would _____ this practice.

  For your _____, we usually _____ insurance _____ the PICC for 110% of the invoice value.

  We hope that you will _____ to our suggestion and look forward to your favorable reply.

Your faithfully,

III. Translate the following sentences into English.

1. 请按发票金额的110%投保一切险和战争险。
2. 根据合同条款，该批货物由买方自行投保。
3. 我公司可以承保海洋运输的所有险别。
4. 如果投保附加险，附加费用由买方承担。
5. 保险责任的起讫期限有多长？

IV. Writing practice.

1. Write a letter to your American customer, explaining to him what kind of coverage you'll arrange for him for the ordered Men's Shirts. Tell him that you accept his request for insuring the goods at the invoice value plus 20%, but the premium for the difference between 120% and 110% of the invoice value should be borne by him.

2. Write a letter about confirmation of terms of packing (open).

Supplement

 Supplementary Reading

1. Letter 1: Inquiring About Insurance Rate

Dear Sir or Madam,

  We will send a consignment of 1,000 sets of typewriters to New York. The consignment is to be loaded on the S. S. "Dong Feng" which sails from Tsinan on July.

Situation 6 Shipment and Insurance

Details with regard to packing and values are attached, and we would be grateful if you could quote a rate covering the All Risks.

A prompt reply will be appreciated.

Yours sincerely,

2. Letter 2: Reply to the Above

Dear Sirs,

Thank you for your letter of May 26 asking us to quote a rate covering the All Risks.

The premium to this cover is at the rate of 0.65% of the declared value of USD 125,000.

This is an exceptionally low rate and we trust you will be satisfied with it and give us the opportunity to handle your insurance business. We are ready to assist you at any time on all future insurance contracts.

Yours faithfully,

3. Background of Ocean Cargo Insurance in International Trade

Ocean cargo insurance is concerned primarily with international commerce. Basically, anyone who has an insurable interest in a cargo shipment (i.e., anyone who would suffer a loss if the cargo were damaged or destroyed or who would benefit from the safe arrival of the cargo) has a need for an ocean cargo policy. The cargo insurance policy indemnifies the exporter or importer in the event of loss or damage to goods due to a peril insured against while at risk under the policy.

Historically, each voyage of an ocean-going vessel is a joint venture of the ship owner and all the cargo owners. Centuries of tradition, trade practice, maritime and international commercial law affect the interests of the international trader.

Cargo insurance protection is an aid to commercial negotiations. It allows traders to proceed with confidence in the knowledge that each party to the transaction is properly protected. In most cases the cost of marine insurance is nominal when compared with the value of the goods and the freight cost.

The marine cargo insurance policy can be designed to meet the individual needs of the exporter or importer in an international transaction.

This insurance is classified into the following three conditions Free From Particular Average (FPA), With Particular Average (WPA) and All Risks.

4. Terms Involved

The Insurant / Insured/Assured

The party that buys insurance (exporter/importer).

The Insurer

The party undertaking to indemnify the insurant against losses or damages (PICC).

The Claimant

The claimant may not necessarily be the insurant.

The Insurance Policy

The contract made between the insurer and the insured.

The Insured Amount

The amount covered against the subject matter (which is usually the amount of 110% of CIF value of the consignment).

Premium

The sum of money the insured agrees to pay the insurer for an insurance policy.

Insurance Documents

Commonly used insurance documents in international trade.

(1) Insurance policy (保单): the mostly used insurance document.

(2) Insurance certificate (保险凭证): a simplified insurance document. The certificate carries the same contents as the insurance policy except for the obligations and rights of the insurer and the insured.

(3) Combined certificate (联合凭证): the combination of the invoice and insurance policy, much simpler than the insurance certificate. It is not often used now.

(4) Open policy (预约保单): also known as open cover, the general contract between the insured (normally the importer) and the insurer, often used in import transactions in China.

(5) Endorsement (批单): after the insurance policy is issued, if the insured wants to add or change some items of the policy, the insured can, with the insurance company's consent, apply for the addition and change. The document issued to state the additional items or changes is known as endorsement, which is considered an indispensable part to the policy.

✓ Knowledge Link

☆ 保险条款

我国在国际贸易中使用最多的两种保险条款为:

1.《中国保险条款》(*China Insurance Clauses*, CIC)

该条款是由中国人民保险公司制定,中国人民银行及中国保险监督委员会审批颁布。根据中国保险条款,海洋保险基本险别有三种:

1) 平安险(Free from Particular Average, FPA)。

2）水渍险（With Particular Average, WPA）。

3）一切险/综合险（All Risks）。

2.《协会货物条款》(*Institute Cargo Clauses*, ICC)

该条款由伦敦保险协会制定，是国际保险市场上普遍采用的条款。

《协会货物条款》共有六种险别，它们是：

1）协会货物条款（A），简称 ICC（A）

2）协会货物条款（B），简称 ICC（B）

3）协会货物条款（C），简称 ICC（C）

4）协会战争险条款（货物），简称 IWCC

5）协会罢工险条款（货物），简称 ISCC

6）恶意损害险（Malicious Damage Clause）

在以上六种险别中，ICC（A）相当于中国保险条款中的一切险，其责任范围更为广泛，故采用承保"除外责任"之外的一切风险的方式表明其承保范围。ICC（B）大体上相当于水渍险。ICC（C）相当于平安险，但承保范围较小。ICC（B）和 ICC（C）都采用列明风险的方式表示其承保范围。六种险别中只有恶意损害险属于附加险别，不能单独投保，其他五种险别的结构相同，体系完整。

Sum-Up

The following sentences are usually used in business letters concerning packing, shipment and insurance.

1. Giving Packing Instructions

◇ The socks should be packed in boxes of 12 pairs each, 10 boxes into a carton.

袜子要装在纸盒里，每盒12双，每10盒装一个纸箱。

◇ On the outer packing, please mark wording "Handle with Care".

在外包装上请标明"小心轻放"字样。

◇ Regarding shipping marks, please stencil our initials in a diamond.

关于唛头，请将我公司首字母缩写刷在一个菱形内。

2. Giving Shipping Instructions

◇ Shipment is to be made in three equal monthly lots beginning from June.

装运应从六月份开始，分三个月平均装运。

◇ Please ship the goods under contract by S. S. …

请将合同项下的货物通过……货轮装运。

◇ The above order is in urgent need, therefore we insist upon express shipment.

因急需上列订单的商品，故我方要求使用快运。

3. Urging Shipment

◇ As the goods are urgently needed, we should be glad if you would dispatch them without further delay.

因为急需这批货物,望即刻发货不再拖延。

◇ We sent you the L/C 20 days ago, but till now we haven't received any information from your company about shipment.

信用证已于20天前寄给你方,但到目前为止,我方未收到任何有关装运的信息。

4. Asking for Partial Shipment or Transshipment

◇ As there is no direct steamer, shipment has to be made by an indirect steamer with transshipment at Hong Kong.

由于没有直达船,货物只好用非直达船装运,在香港转船。

◇ Shall we ship the first 50 tons in May and the balance in the following month?

我们能否在5月份先装运50吨,剩余的下个月装?

5. Making Shipping Advice

◇ We have shipped the goods on S.S. "Chang Ji" which is estimated to reach your port on May 12.

我们已将货物装上"昌吉号"轮,预计到达你方港口时间为5月12日。

◇ The consignment has been shipped on June 21.

货物已于6月21日装运。

6. Discussing Insurance Details

◇ Please cover the insurance at your end.

请在你处投保。

◇ For the sake of safety, we recommend you to insure against All Risks and War Risk.

为安全起见,我们建议你方为这批货物投保一切险和战争险。

◇ We usually effect insurance against All Risks for full invoice value plus 10% for the goods sold on CIF basis.

对于按CIF出售的货物,我们通常按发票金额的110%投保一切险。

◇ Should additional risks be covered, the extra premium is for buyer's account.

如果要投保附加险,额外的保费由买方负担。

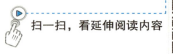

Situation 07

Complaints and Claim

📝 Objectives

1) Be able to translate and write a letter of complaints and reply.
2) To be able to translate and write a letter of claims and settlement.

📝 Introduction

In international trade, complaints and claims often happen because of shortage of quantity, the delivery of wrong goods, delay of delivery and improper packing, etc.

A claim letter is a demand from a customer for something that is due or owed, or something that is a correction of a problem. Complaints and claims are usually raised by buyers. However, sellers may also raise claims against buyers for non-establishments of L/C or breach of contract, etc. A claim should be made as quickly as possible for it can be rejected if it is too late.

After receiving the complaints or claims, the counterpart will make an immediate investigation and settle the problem as soon as possible. That is called the adjustment.

Main Points of Complaints or Claims

1) Referring to the relative goods or shipment.
2) Stating the problem suffered in details and presenting the loss or inconvenience.
3) Proposing the way of settlement, such as request for replacement, delivery or compensation.
4) Showing the wish of prompt attention or early reply.

Main Points of Replies

1) Showing receipt of the letter and regret at the complaint or claim.

2) a. Stating acceptance of the claim or agreement to the settlement.

   b. Stating disagreement to the complaint or claim and showing the reason.

3) Showing expectation for future business.

Task ❶ Complaints and Reply

Preparing

Relative Reading

Introductory Remark

In business, if the buyer can prove that it is the seller's responsibility for the loss of the goods, he can make a claim. The seller is obligated to compensate the buyer. Generally speaking, claims arise because the wrong goods may have been delivered; the quality may have been found unsatisfactory; the shipment may have been found damaged, short, missing, late; the prices charged may be excessive or not as agreed.

There is also another kind of claim. It is made by buyers who find fault with the goods as an excuse to escape from the contract, either because they no longer want the goods or because that they can get them cheaper elsewhere.

If a claim has to be made by the buyer, the matter should be investigated in detail and these details should be laid before the party charged. We must handle claims with the principle of "on the first grounds, to our advantage and with restraint" and settle them amicably to the satisfaction of all parties concerned.

What is Complaint?

A statement that a situation is unsatisfactory or unacceptable or that someone has done something wrong. In business activities, no matter how perfect an organization may be, complaints from the customers are certain to arise.

Rules for Writing Complaints and Claims

1) Begin immediately and clearly. Tell what is wrong.

2) Identify the situation (invoice, product information, etc.) in the text. Describe the story in a clear and organized way.

3) Present enough facts to permit a decision.

4) Name specific actions to correct the problem and politely mention strong terms if you

fail to get a satisfactory reply.

5) End positively—friendly but firm.

How to Write a Letter of Complaint?

1) The most important rule is to avoid rudeness or sarcasm.

2) Complain timely.

3) State the fact clearly and keep the letter short.

Staging of the Letter of Complaint

First, state the background of the complaint.

Then raise the issue.

Suggest a solution.

State possible action.

Tips for Effective Complaints

1) Complain as soon as possible.

2) Find out about your legal rights. Are there any laws or regulations that can help you?

3) Pay attention to all printed information you have about the case, such as ads, brochure, warranty, or other document that describes the product or service.

4) Talk to the right people, in the right order.

5) Be clear. Know your facts — preferably by keeping a file with all the necessary documents — and use them to ask for what you want.

6) Be polite. You'll get better, and maybe quicker, results if you explain the problem and ask for a resolution without resorting to anger or threats.

7) Be prepared to negotiate realistically.

8) Keep good records. Note the names of people you talk to, as well as the dates, times and outcomes of the conversations.

9) It's often best to explain the problem in writing.

10) Always keep a copy of each letter you write for your own files.

Parties Involved in the Claim and Settlement Process

Ship owner; charters; freight forwarders; airlines, inland trucking companies; rail companies; shippers; insurance companies.

Parties Involved in Insurance

Seller, buyer, carrier and insurer.

Documents Generally Required for Making a Claim Against an Insurance Company or Shipping Company

1) Survey Report（检验报告）
2) Certificate of Inspection（检验证书）
3) Mate's Receipt（大副收据）
4) Invoice（发票）
5) Insurance Policy（保险单）
6) Weight Certificate（重量证明）
7) Marine Protect（海难证明书）
8) Packing List（装箱单）
9) Shortlanded Certificate（短卸证明书）
10) Damage Report（破损证明）
11) Weight Note（磅码单）
12) Tally-List（理货单）

Common Causes for Complaints and Claims in International Trade

✓ Lead In — Dialogues

Mr. Zhang Lin（A）is now talking with his ball-pen supplier Mr. Smith（B）about the three hundred faulty pens they've just purchased.

A: Mr. Smith, we have always been able to rely on the high quality of your ball-pens. They are very popular with our customers. But this time I'm afraid we won't be able to sell them.

B: Why on earth not? Do you mean there is something wrong with our pens?

A: Mr. Smith, that's just the trouble. Our customers say they fail to write without rubbing,

Situation 7　Complaints and Claim

and some of the pens leak.

B: But how can that be? Every batch of pens was checked before being sent out.

A: This order was placed according to your sample pen. We have compared the performance of the sample with these pens and found many of them faulty.

B: All our ball-pens are produced to identical standards in design and performance. It seems impossible that those sold to your customers should have given trouble.

A: But you have all facts before you. Here are the pens we brought with us.

B: Maybe they escaped the examination we normally give to all pens.

A: Do you mean the fault lies with your inspection department?

B: I am afraid so.

A: In that case, now what will you do to help us get over this difficulty?

B: Do the faulty pens form a large part of the consignment?

A: Yes, about three hundred out of two thousand.

B: Well, to simplify the matter, we will get these pens replaced by new ones straight away.

A: I was just going to suggest that.

Performing

Text

Sample 1　Complaint About Wrong Delivery

Dear Mr. Wang,

　　We have received our Order No. for Canon digital cameras. On opening the cases we noticed that we had received the wrong goods. We received IXUS 60 instead of IXUS 75 that we ordered.

　　Please advise us when we can expect to receive our order. And we could like to know what we should do with the items now in our possession.

Yours sincerely,
Mary
ABC Co. Ltd.

Sample 2　Reply to the Above

Dear Mrs. Green,

　　We have received your letter dated July 23 informing us of the wrong delivery of digital cameras.

On going into the matter we find that a mistake was indeed made in packing, through a confusion of number. We have arranged for the right goods to be dispatched to you at once. Relative documents will be mailed as soon as possible.

As to the items that you have received, we hope that you will be willing to keep those and if they will be popular with your customers. If they don't move you can return them to us. In any event, we will pay all shipping charges.

Yours sincerely,
Wang Ning
Green Star Imp. and Exp. Co. Ltd.

Sample 3 Complaint About Delay of Supplies

Dear Mr Smith,

Order No. 68197

I am writing to inform you that the goods we ordered from your company have not been supplied correctly.

On 15 June 2017 we placed an order with your firm for 12,000 ultra super long-life batteries. The consignment arrived yesterday but contained only 1,200 batteries.

This error put our firm in a difficult position, as we had to make some emergency purchases to fulfill our commitments to all our customers. This caused us considerable inconvenience.

I am writing to ask you to please make up the shortfall immediately and to ensure that such errors do not happen again. Otherwise, we may have to look elsewhere for our supplies.

I look forward to hearing from you by return.

Yours sincerely,
Bob

Notes

1) complaint   *n.* an expression of dissatisfaction   抱怨，起诉，申诉

　　lodge / make / lay a complaint against…   对……提出申诉

　　　e. g. We received a complaint about short weight.

　　　　　　我们收到一份对短重的申诉。

　　complain   *v.* 投诉

　　　e. g. Many customers complain about the products.

　　　　　　许多客户投诉该产品。

Situation 7　Complaints and Claim

2) in our possession　我方手头的货

3) go into　look into, investigate　调查

  e. g. After going into the matter, we find damage was caused by careless handling at the dock.
  经调查，损坏系码头作业不小心所致。

4) move　sell well　卖得出

5) in any event　in any case　不管怎样，无论如何

  e. g. In any event, we will arrange the shipment before the end of this month.
  不管怎样，我们会在本月底前安排装运。

Practicing

I. Translate the following expressions into English.

申诉　　　　　　　　索赔
错装　　　　　　　　调查
不管怎样　　　　　　保留索赔的权利
我方手头的货　　　　短装
卖得出　　　　　　　对……提出申诉

II. Fill in the blanks with proper prepositions.

1. We have lodged a claim _____ ABC Co. _____ the quality of the goods shipped _____ S. S. "Peace".

2. The quality is not in conformity _____ the agreed specifications.

3. We have dispatched the goods _____ the same quality to many other houses.

4. We find it imperative to look _____ the matter as soon as possible.

5. As arranged, we have effected insurance _____ the goods _____ 130% of the invoice value _____ All Risks.

6. We regret to have to complain _____ the short-weight of the goods.

III. Translate the following sentences into Chinese

1. We require you to replace the goods with perfect goods.

2. We regret to know that you did not receive the ten sets of Sony TV sets you ordered.

3. On examination, we have found not all the goods correspond with your original samples.

4. To our great surprise, we find the goods are far below the standard stipulated in the contract.

5. Any complaint about the quality of the products should be lodged within 15 days after

arrival.

IV. Translate the following into English.

1. Translate the following letter into English.

敬启者：

贵公司于7月18日来信投诉由"幸运号"转运的棉花出现问题，本公司非常遗憾。经调查，证实该批货物离岸时完好无缺，提单可做证明。显然你方所投诉的损失是发生于运输途中，因此本公司不对此损失负责。

本公司建议贵公司向船公司或保险公司索赔。

盼能尽早解决有关问题。

谨上

2. Translate the following sentences into English.

1) 说实话我并不喜欢投诉，可你们公司总是给我带来这样那样的麻烦。我找过你们许多部门，但无济于事。这次我要直接找你们领导反映。

2) 目前恐怕我们还没有办法解决此事，但我会在一两天内给您答复。

3) 他的话听起来似乎有些道理，但我们还是应该找出错误的真正原因。

4) 我们没有要这种货物是由于它的价格不合适，更不用说其质量差。

5) 得知此事给你们带来如此多的不便，我们的供货商也非常难过。

V. Writing Practice.

1. Write a letter to complain about late delivery / inferior or wrong quality/shortage of goods/poor packing.

2. Write a letter to complain about the wrong goods.

Supplement

Supplementary Reading

1. Letter: Complaints About Short Delivery

Dear Sirs,

We received on June 13 three cases of goods under our Order No. 859. Upon examination of the goods against your invoice, we discovered a shortage in number of Apple MP3. whereas 500 sets were ordered, we received only 400 sets.

The cases are intact. The shortage may be due to confusion in packing. And we notify you that we reserve the right to claim on you for the shortage.

Please investigate this matter carefully and ship the additional 100 sets of Apple MP3 on the earliest possible flight from California at your expense.

Yours faithfully,

2. Complaint Letters

A complaint letter requests some sort of compensation for defective or damaged merchandise or for inadequate or delayed services. While many complaints can be made in person, some circumstances require formal business letters. The complaint may be so complex that a phone call may not effectively resolve the problem; or the writer may prefer the permanence, formality, and seriousness of a business letter. The essential rule in writing a complaint letter is to maintain your poise and diplomacy, no matter how justified your gripe is. Avoid making the recipient an adversary.

1) **Identify Early the Reason You Are Writing** — to register a complaint and to ask for some kind of compensation. Avoid leaping into the details of the problem in the first sentence.

2) **State Exactly What Compensation You Desire**, either before or after the discussion of the problem or the reasons for granting the compensation.

3) **Provide a Fully Detailed Narrative or Description of the Problem**. This is the "evidence".

4) **Explain Why Your Request Should be Granted.** Presenting the evidence is not enough: state the reasons why this evidence indicates your request should be granted.

5) **Suggest Why it is in the Recipient's Best Interest to Grant Your Request**: appeal to the recipient's sense of fairness, desire for continued business, but don't threaten. Find some way to view the problem as an honest mistake. Don't imply that the recipient deliberately committed the error or that the company has no concern for the customer. Toward the end of the letter, express confidence that the recipient will grant your request.

3. Adjustment Letters

Replies to complaint letters, often called letters of "adjustment", must be handled carefully when the requested compensation cannot be granted. Refusal of compensation tests your diplomacy and tact as a writer. Some suggestions as follows:

1) Begin with a reference to the date of the original letter of complaint and to the purpose of your letter. If you deny the request, don't state the refusal right away unless you can do so tactfully.

2) Express your concern over the writer's troubles and your appreciation that he has

written you.

3) If you deny the request, explain the reasons why the request cannot be granted in as cordial manner as possible. If you grant the request, don't sound as if you are doing so in a begrudging way.

4) If you deny the request, try to offer some partial or substitute compensation or offer some friendly advice.

5) Conclude the letter cordially, perhaps expressing confidence that you and the writer will continue doing business.

Knowledge Link

☆ 佳能数码照相机

佳能是全球领先的生产影像与信息产品的综合集团。自 1937 年成立以来，佳能将自己的业务全球化并扩展到各个领域。目前，佳能的产品系列共分布于三大领域：个人产品、办公设备和工业设备，主要产品包括照相机及镜头、数码相机、打印机、复印机、传真机、扫描仪、广播设备、医疗器材及半导体生产设备等。佳能总部位于日本东京，并在美洲、欧洲、亚洲及日本设有四大区域性销售总部，在世界各地拥有子公司 200 多家，雇员超过 10 万人。

Task 2 Claims and Settlement

Preparing

Relative Reading

What is Claim?

An application for compensation under the terms of an insurance policy. Handle complaints or claims in accordance with the principle of "on the first grounds, to our advantage and with restraint".

The Reasons for Claims

Shortage (short weight) 短重
Breakage 破碎
Leakage 渗漏
Damage 损坏
Improper/faulty packing 不良包装
Inferior quality 不良品质

Delay 延误

Types of Claims Frequently Filed by Importers & Exporters

- Inferior quality
- Quality discrepancy
- Poor packing
- Damage
- Shortage
- Delayed shipment
- Unreasonable rejection of the goods
- Did not open an L/C in time
- Loss of the goods
- Wrong delivery

Documents Required When Lodging a Claim

- Original Insurance Policy or Insurance Certificate
- Contract of Affreightment
- Commercial Invoice, Weight Memo
- Packing List
- Survey Report
- Certificate of Loss or Damage
- Any correspondence with the carrier or any other party who could be responsible for the loss or damage.

Ways to Resolve Disputes

There are four ways to resolve a dispute between the seller and the buyer in international trade:

negotiation（协商）
conciliation（调解）
arbitration（仲裁）
litigation（诉讼）

✓ Lead In — Dialogues

The seller has sent one container of different computers ordered by the buyer, which makes the buyer suffer a loss of nearly USD 30,000. So the buyer lodged a claim of USD 30,000 against the seller, who sent a representative, Mr. Parton to China to carry out an on-the-pot inspection and settle the claim with Mr. Wu, the representative of the buyer.

A: Welcome to our company, Mr. Parton. I'm Wu Ming, the manager in charge of the import department.

B: Nice to meet you, Mr. Wu. I'm assigned to settle the claim you lodged against us for our shipping wrong goods. I'm sure that we can clear up this matter through personal discussion.

A: I hope so. We are very sorry to have filed a complaint about the wrong goods you shipped to us.

B: I have to make a careful investigation of the case first. Would you please state the facts?

A: When we opened each carton in Container No. 16, we found it contained completely different articles. We had taken the goods into our warehouse.

B: What articles were contained in Container No. 16?

A: The COMPAQ KA2 type computers. Let's go to the warehouse and have a look.

B: I believe what you said. We needn't go to the warehouse. Let's discuss how to settle the case.

A: Owing to the loss, we just claim for USD 30,000 against you. What's your opinion?

B: We regret sending you the wrong goods. But one container of wrong goods would not make you suffer so much loss. Your claim of USD 30,000 is unacceptable.

A: In fact, the loss caused by shipping wrong goods is more than USD 30,000, but for the sake of friendship, we only lodge a claim of USD 30,000.

B: Mr. Wu, as we know, the price difference between the two types of computer is only USD 12,000.

A: But, Mr. Parton, this price difference can't represent our loss caused by your shipping the wrong goods. Many of our customers complained about the delay in supplying their orders. Some of them even canceled their orders. Besides, we can't sell the wrong goods you shipped to our customers without your consent.

B: We understand your problem, and regret for bringing you the troubles. Well, Mr. Wu, if you can help us to sell the goods in Container No. 16, we'll compensate you USD 30,000. What's your opinion?

A: OK, that's the deal.

Performing

✓ Text

Sample 1 Claim for Short Weight

Dear Sirs,

Re: Our Order No. 234 for 10 M/T Chemical Fertilizer

Situation 7　Complaints and Claim

We have just received the Survey Report from Shanghai Entry-Exit Inspection and Quarantine Bureau evidencing that the captioned goods unloaded here yesterday was short weight 1,120 kgs. A thorough inspection showed that the short weight was due to the improper packing, for which the suppliers should be definitely responsible.

On the basis of the Survey Report, we hereby register a claim with you for GBP 270 in all.

We are enclosing the Survey Report No. 118 and look forward to your settlement at an early date.

Yours faithfully,

Sample 2　Settlement of the Above Claim

Dear Sirs,

With reference to your Claim No. 145 for short weight of 1,120 kgs. of Chemical Fertilizer, we wish to express our much regret over the unfortunate incident.

After a check-up by our staff, it was found that some 28 bags had not been packed in 5-ply strong paper bags as stipulated in the contract, thus resulting in the breakage during transit, for which we tender our apologies.

In view of our long-standing business relations, we will make payment by cheque for GBP 270, the amount of claim, into your account with Bank of China, upon receipt of your agreement.

We trust that the arrangement we have made will satisfy you and look forward to receiving your further orders.

Yours faithfully,

Sample 3　Claims for Poor Packing

Dear Sirs,

We are regretful to inform you that the Poplin covered by our Order No. 5413 and shipped per S. S. "Queen" arrived in such an unsatisfactory condition that we have to lodge a claim against you. It was found upon examination that nearly 30% of the packages had been broken, obviously due to insufficient packing. The only recourse in consequence, was to have them repacked before delivering to our customers, which inevitably resulted in extra expenses amounting to USD 765. We trust you understand the inconvenience caused by it and meanwhile expect your compensation for this.

We should like to remind that special care be taken in your future deliveries for prospective customers are liable to misjudge the quality of your goods by the poor packing.

Yours faithfully,

Notes

1) short weight   短重，也可写作 shortweight 或 short-weight

   e.g. We lodge a claim against you for a short weight of 4.6 M/T.
   我方为短重4.6吨向你方提出索赔。

   short   *adj.* inadequate, insufficient   不足，缺少

   short weight   短重

   short shipment   短装

   short invoiced   发票少开的

   short shipped   短装的

   be in short supply   供应短缺

2) inspection   *n.* the act of checking, examining   检验，检查

   commodity inspection   商品检验

   Inspection Certificate   检验证书

   inspect   *v.* 检验，检查

   e.g. Upon arrival of the goods at out port we had them immediately reinspected.
   货物到达我方港口，我方立即重新检验了货物。

3) claim   *n.* demand for payment, request   索赔，赔偿要求

   lodge/ register/ file a claim against/ with sb. for/ on sth. 因某种原因向某人索赔

   e.g. We are entitled to lodge a claim for the inferior quality against the seller.
   我们有权因货物质量低劣向卖方索赔。

4) settlement   *n.* conclusion, payment   解决，清偿

   in settlement of   用以清偿，解决

   settle   *v.* 解决，清偿

   settle claims   理赔

   settle an account   结算账户

5) check-up   *n.* 检查，检验

6) 5-ply   五层

   ply   *n.* 厚度，层片

   three-ply wood   三夹板，三合板

   a two-ply rope   一根双股的绳子

   e.g. The cartons should be strengthened by two-ply nylon straps.
   纸箱必须用双股尼龙带加固。

Situation 7 Complaints and Claim

Practicing

I. Translate the following expressions into Chinese.

survey report
short weight
lodge a claim
insurance policy
settle an account

CIQ
commodity inspection
three-ply wood
settle claims
be in short supply

II. Fill in the blanks with the following words or expressions.

| settlement | agree to | lodge | took delivery of | alternative |

1. The inferior quality of your shipment causes us to _____ the claim.
2. On arrival of M. V. "Castle" at Port Louis, we _____ the consignment.
3. We have no _____ but to ask for compensation to cover our loss.
4. Amicable _____ of a dispute is preferable to a law suit.
5. If your business with us turns out to our satisfaction, we will _____ renew the agency agreement.

III. Complete the following sentences by translating Chinese into English.

1. In view of the long-standing business relations between us, _____ _____ (我们希望友好解决争议).
2. _____ (我们没有别的办法，只能把货退回), or we'll cancel the contract.
3. _____ (这批货估计短重500公斤), but we are still waiting for the survey report.
4. On strength of the contract, the buyer _____ _____ (有权退货并提出索赔).
5. We consider that _____ (供应商应该为短装负责任) because 30 bags were found broken when unloading.

IV. Writing Practice.

1. Write a letter of claim to the supplier stating the following points.

   1) 订单123号60箱家用器皿货物收到。
   2) 其中8只箱子破裂，内装器皿损坏。
   3) 检验报告证明损坏系不良包装所致。
   4) 要求赔偿损失费及检验费共计金额……。

2. Write a letter of claim to the supplier for short-weight and inferior quality on the consignment of Rice shipped per S. S. "Green Trees" —Contract No. DG 3109—Rice.

Supplement

Supplementary Reading

1. Letter 1: Claim Against an Insurance Company

Dear Sirs,

We are holders of Insurance Policy No. 5678 issued by your company on 1,000 cases of toys valued at USD 15,600. The ship encountered heavy weather, and 150 cases were damaged by sea water. We are enclosing the Survey Report, also the Policy, which is against WPA.

Your prompt attention will be appreciated.

Yours faithfully,

2. Letter 2: Claims Against a Shipping Company

Dear Sirs,

1,000 sets of Color Television under Order No. 3345 per S. S. "Yellow River" on June 23 arrived here yesterday.

On examination, we have found that many of the Color Televisions are severely damaged.

Considering this damage was due to improper packing by the exporter, we claimed on them for recovery of the loss; but an investigation made by the surveyor has revealed the fact that the damage is attributable to the rough handling. For further particulars, we refer you to the surveyor's report enclosed.

We are therefore, compelled to claim on you to compensate us for the loss, USD 80,000, which we have sustained by the damage to the goods.

We trust that you will be kind enough to accept this claim.

Yours truly,

3. Basic Knowledge

In international trade, most complaints or claims are made by buyers against sellers for the losses. However, there are times when claims made by sellers against buyers. Though the parties to a sales contract are the seller and the buyer, the claim-settlement procedures may include other parties such as shipping companies (carrier), insurance companies, etc. So they may also be responsible for the losses or damages in some cases.

4. The Seller is Responsible for the Following:

- Non-delivery or partial delivery
- Delay in delivery/shipment
- Inferior quality
- Wrong quantity
- Insufficient packing
- Failure in entering into contract
- Non-fulfillment of contract
- Discrepancies in specifications

5. The Buyer is Responsible for the Following:

- Refuse to open an L/C
- Delay in opening L/C
- Delay in payment
- Commission unpaid
- Failure in entering into contract
- Non-fulfillment of contract

6. The Carrier is Responsible for the Following:

- Short-landed
- Goods missing
- Rough handling
- Others

7. The Insurer is Responsible for the Following:

- Goods suffer losses or damages in transit because of the risks insured against.
- Other reasons stipulated in the policy according to which, the insured is entitled to ask for compensation.

✓ Knowledge Link

☆ 中华人民共和国海关总署

中华人民共和国海关是国家的进出关境（简称进出境）监督管理机关，实行垂直管理体制。基本任务是进出境监管、征收关税和其他税费、查缉走私、编制海关统计，并承担口岸管理、保税监管、海关稽查、知识产权海关保护、国际海关合作等职责。

十三届全国人大一次会议审议通过的《国务院机构改革方案》明确"原国家质量监督检验检疫总局的出入境检验检疫管理职责和队伍划入海关总署"。

Sum-Up

The following sentences are usually used in lodging a complaint or claim and making relative settlement.

1. Concerning Details of Problem

- ◇ The goods delivered are not up to the standard of samples. (质量低劣)
  所交货物未达到样品的质量标准。
- ◇ We regret to inform you that 8 cartons were broken. (不良包装)
  很遗憾地通知贵方,有 8 只纸箱破损。
- ◇ We regret to point out that a shortage in weight of 200 lbs. was noticed when goods arrived. (短重)
  很遗憾,货物到达时我们发现短重 200 磅。
- ◇ Evidently some mistake was made and the goods have been wrongly delivered. (错发货物)
  显然发生了差错,以致错发了货。

2. Making a Complaint or Lodging a Claim

- ◇ As the goods are not identical with the L/C, we can not help cancelling this transaction.
  由于这批货物与信用证不符,我们只好取消交易。
- ◇ We have to file a claim against you on the shipment for short weight for USD 450.
  因短重,我们要向你方就这批货提出索赔,金额 450 美元。

3. Settling the Claim

- ◇ In the spirit of goodwill and friendship, we agree to accept all your claim.
  本着友好精神,我方同意接受你方的全部索赔。
- ◇ We regret for the losses you have suffered and agree to compensate you by USD 1,000.
  对你方所遭受的损失我方深表遗憾,同意赔偿 1,000 美元。
- ◇ It's not our responsibility for the goods in question are in good condition when they left here, which can be evidenced by the B/L.
  这不是我方的责任,因为货物离岸时状况良好,有提单为证。
- ◇ Your claim should be referred to the shipping company or the insurance company.
  你方应向船公司或者保险公司索赔。

Situation 7　Complaints and Claim

4. Poor Quality

◇ To our surprise, we found the goods are far below the standard and didn't meet the sample.
使我们吃惊的是，我们发现货物远达不到标准，比样品差远了。

◇ We found the quality of the goods is not in conformity with what we stipulated in the contract.
我们发现货物质量与合同规定的不一致。

5. Poor Packing

◇ We regret to inform you that Case No. 36 is broken. The contents are seriously damaged owing to improper packing.
很遗憾地通知你方，36号箱子破了。由于包装不当，里面的货物严重受损。

◇ We found 8 cartons were torn and 4 cartons were broken.
我们发现8箱散了，4箱破了。

6. Shortage

◇ We feel it regrettable that only 97 cases were received by us.
很遗憾，我们只收到97箱。

◇ After inspection of the above shipment, we found eight boxes are missing.
我方经检验发现，上述货物中有8箱丢失。

7. Wrong Delivery

◇ Everything appears to be correct and in good condition except in Case No. 40.
除40号箱以外，其他货物正常，状况良好。

◇ When we opened this case we found it contained completely different articles.
当打开这个箱子时，我方发现里面的货物完全不对。

8. Notice of Complaint or Claim

◇ We were glad to know that the consignment was delivered promptly, but it was with much regret that we heard Case No. 40 did not contain the goods you ordered.
得知货物按时运到了，我方很高兴，但当得知40号箱所装货物不是你方订购的货时，我方为此感到遗憾。

◇ We are in receipt of your letter of May 1 claiming for short weight on the consignment of…
收到你方5月1日来信，向我方索赔……的短重。

9. Acceptance of Complaint or Claim

◇ We regret for the losses you have suffered and agree to compensate you by USD

15,000.

对你方所遭受的损失我方深表遗憾，同意赔偿15,000美元。

◇ We are prepared to compensate you by 10% of the total invoice value.

我们打算赔偿你方发票价值的10%。

10. Rejection of Complaint or Claim

◇ Your claim should be referred to the insurance company.

你方应向保险公司索赔。

◇ We looked into the matter and found that our products were properly weighed at the time of loading.

我们调查了此事，认为装运时货物的重量是正确的。

◇ The goods in question were in first-class condition when they left here, as was evidenced by the bill of lading.

该货物离开这里时状况良好，这有提单为证。

参考文献

[1] 虞苏美,张逸. 商务英语精读 [M]. 北京:高等教育出版社,2002.

[2] 孔庆炎,王洗薇. 世纪商务英语综合教程 [M]. 大连:大连理工大学出版社,2007.

[3] 陈威,粟景妆. 世纪商务英语综合教程 [M]. 大连:大连理工大学出版社,2005.

[4] 戚云云. 外经贸英语函电与谈判 [M]. 杭州:浙江大学出版社,2001.

[5] 朱慧萍. 营销英语 [M]. 上海:上海外语教育出版社,2004.

[6] 帕金森. 牛津英汉双解商务英语词典 [M]. 李健,译. 北京:华夏出版社,2004.

[7] 卜玉坤,李来发,等. 管理学英语 [M]. 北京:外语教育与研究出版社,2004.

[8] 陈准民. 工商导论 [M]. 北京:高等教育出版社,2004.

[9] 罗虹,陆志兴. 商务英语选读 [M]. 武汉:武汉大学出版社,2004.

[10] 杨翠萍,谢丹焰,邱丕杰. 商务英语综合教程 [M]. 北京:清华大学出版社,北方交通大学出版社,2002.

[11] 褚志梅. 商务英语精读 [M]. 北京:清华大学出版社,北京交通大学出版社,2003.

[12] 师英,周红. 国际商务英文读本 [M]. 天津:南开大学出版社,2003.

[13] 陈苏东,陈建平,赵军峰. 商务英语口译 [M]. 北京:高等教育出版社,2004.

[14] 杨文慧,周瑞琪. 商务礼仪英语 [M]. 广州:中山大学出版社,2003.

[15] 陈怡平. 现学现用商务英语 [M]. 北京:外文出版社,2004.

[16] 马麟,孙健. 外贸接单员高效工作手册 [M]. 北京:人民邮电出版社,2008.

[17] 爱德华G. 辛克尔曼. 国际贸易英英、英汉双解词典 [M]. 李健,译. 北京:经济科学出版社,2002.

[18] 何兆熊. 当代商务英语综合教程 [M]. 上海:华东师范大学出版社,2008.

[19] 任书梅,王璐. 商务英语入门 [M]. 北京:外语教学与研究出版社,2005.

[20] 科顿,法维尔,肯特. 体验商务英语综合教程 [M]. 北京:高等教育出版社,2005.

[21] 余慕鸿,章汝雯. 商务英语谈判 [M]. 北京:外语教学与研究出版社,2005.

[22] 剑桥大学考试委员会,剑桥BEC真题集(初级、中级、高级) [M]. 北京:人民邮电出版社,2005.

[23] 马斯卡尔. 新剑桥商务英语中高级词汇用法 [M]. 北京:人民邮电出版社,2005.

[24] 冯祥春,隋思忠. 大学外贸英语自学手册 [M]. 北京:中国对外经济贸易大学出版社,2002.

[25] 凌华倍,朱佩芬. 外经贸英语函电与谈判 [M]. 北京:中国对外经济贸易出版社,2002.

[26] 荣民,尹得永. 涉外经贸法律英语 [M]. 北京:首都经济贸易大学出版社,2000.

[27] 黄锡光,吴宝康. 国际贸易实务 [M]. 上海:复旦大学出版社,2006.

[28] 许葵花. 国贸际易英语教程 [M]. 西安:西安交通大学出版社,2004.

[29] 卓新光. 国际贸易英语 [M]. 长春:吉林人民出版社,2005.

[30] 陶菁. 国际贸易专业英语 [M]. 北京:中国纺织出版社,2008.

[31] 曹菱. 外贸英语实务 [M]. 北京:外语教学与研究出版社,2005.

[32] 邹勇. 国际商务英语——理论与实务 [M]. 上海:上海财经大学出版社,2008.

[33] 尹雅娟,厉秀仁. 国际经贸英语——阅读听说教程 [M]. 北京:知识出版社,2002.

[34] 马丽. 商务英语选读 [M]. 上海:上海外语教育出版社,2001.

[35] 李庆明. 跨文化交际——理论与实践 [M]. 西安:西北工业大学出版社,2007.